All Because of a Love Note

How I unwittingly penned my way into the heart of an epic love
story while writing thousands of love notes to America's heroes

By

Natalie June Reilly

Based on a true Love Note story.

Cover design by Natalie June Reilly
Edited by Natalie June Reilly

To contact Natalie, please send snail mail to:

Natalie June Reilly
P.O. Box 647
Carlsbad, CA 92018

Catch up with her via email at girlwriter68@hotmail.com.

#nothingbutlovenotes

Enjoy!
Book rec by Artist
from Enanitas that
Did the coaster!

For Mom

Tonight ... we ride.

To a
Steady recovery
Love Sis

1/10/2023

gratitude becomes you!

♡

xo,
Natalie ♡

My dear daughter,

Well, looks like 2017 is the year our roles changed, and if so, you make a darn good mother. Thank you for all you've done these last two years, from all the trips to the doctor, from running to the store to get me a fudgesicle, to picking me up when I fell. Stay on the road less traveled and suddenly you will come upon your treasure. So proud of you.

Your fellow minion,
Mom

Author's "Love Note" to Reader
Love is an Inside Job

I was the kid voted "Biggest Dreamer" in the eighth grade by my homeroom class. As a 14-year-old wallflower, I was mortified. I would much rather have been voted "Best Legs" or "Life of the Party," like the cool kids. Only now, four decades later, do I realize, if not appreciate the virtue of being named "Biggest Dreamer." Since a girl's legs have a relatively short shelf life and being the life of the party becomes less attractive with middle-age, I am good with the middle-school moniker. The truth is my pubescent peers got it right. Even now, I am nothing, if not still *the* world's biggest dreamer, one of the last eternal optimists who still believes in God, true love, miracles, the kindness of strangers and the promise of a paperclip.

Allow me to elaborate.

A few years ago, about the same time Nothing but Love Notes was taking off, my firstborn son, Billy, was returning home from deployment in the Persian Gulf aboard the USS Philippine Sea. He was about to be released from the United States Navy and was in the process of becoming a police officer in the state of Georgia. He called me one day from Jacksonville, Florida, asking me to send him all the necessary documents, including his birth certificate, high school diploma, shot records—the works. As I was driving to the post office to drop all these important papers in the mail, I was praying for a paperclip, lest one or more of these documents get lost.

"My kingdom for a paperclip!" I exclaimed.

As I pulled into the packed post office parking lot, I managed to secure the last available parking space in front of the building. I opened up my car door and, lo and behold, there it was—a big, silver paperclip, glinting in the sun at my feet. It was as if the Universe winked at me, placed my order and, with Amazon-like speed, delivered the paperclip in record time. I picked it up, fastened it to the papers and dropped the bundle (along with the gifted paperclip) in the mail. It was divine intervention and just in the nick of time, too. It was also affirmation. That is to say, if you want something from this life, ASK for it. BELIEVE for it, and then put your best foot forward and GO for it.

And then you wait for it.

Ever since that day, paperclips of every shape, size and color have continued to show up in my path—at the grocery store, in parking lots, on sidewalks across America, in airplane terminals, on airplanes, on the beach, in parks, in coffee shops, in truck stops, in bathrooms, in police cars and elevators. You name it. I have found a paperclip there. I've made a habit of picking them up and keeping them in a big, glass container at home that is now filled with hundreds of them, if not thousands. My friends and family have even started finding them and collecting them for me. Like breadcrumbs,

I see each paperclip as a sign from above that I am on the right path.

I know it sounds silly, but when the road gets long and life comes at you sideways, evermore serious and uncertain, this bread-crumb trail of paperclips reinforces my faith. It makes me smile and, if nothing else, it reminds me that God is at the helm. All I can do is follow that which He puts in my path and heart. And when in doubt, there are signs everywhere. You've just got to look for them, and when you're not seeing them, ask for them. Believe for them. Once you see the signs, you'll never not see them. It is written: *"What you ask for and what you believe for is already yours,"(Mark 11:24).*

Trust me on this one. I have a two-gallon glass jar full of little, steel-wire messages from Heaven to prove it. Some are perfectly pristine, and some are rusted and bent out of shape, but each one symbolizes that there is something bigger at work, the stuff of miracles. And while we're on the subject of miracles, I am convinced that if a girl has someone in her corner who loves and believes in her, she has everything she needs in this life and beyond. Throw in faith, gratitude and purpose, and she just might have it in her to make the world a little bit brighter than the way she found it. That, in and of itself, is a recipe for a miracle. I know this to be true because I had all those things, beginning with someone who loved and believed in me. And it was in the middle of losing her, in the darkest days of my life, that I was reminded of who I am.

I am a child of God, and I am Hope's daughter. I believe in all things love, and I was put here to spread kindness—one Love Note at a time. I am a grateful, green-eyed pipe dream, whose legs, by the way, still aren't half bad. I am also someone who doesn't take herself or life too seriously, and who took to heart the good counsel of a fortune cookie that read: *"To capture a city, win the hearts of its people."*

God planted a seed in me, and it was in *that* realization that the game changed. Love is an inside job. It begins and ends with you, where you are right now—this minute. To make the world a better and brighter place, you don't need anything more in your arsenal than love, guts, grit and super-cute stationery. On top of which, if you hope to create an extraordinary life, the one you've always dreamed of, you need a fierce amount of faith, focus and fortitude. But keep in mind … all in God's time.

Oh, and if it's peace of mind you seek, you need only the teeth to bite your tongue. Silence is, indeed, golden, especially these days. You have nothing to prove to anybody. Just do good with what you've got. With that, you are infinite—pure stardust, baby! If you don't believe me, keep reading! ☺

My Mother's Daughter

Two words saved my life, two modest but mighty words—**thank you**! Gratitude, along with grit, grace and barrels of ink kept me from losing hope in a really dark time, which is ironic, in and of itself because that's what was happening. I was losing Hope, the woman who brought me into this world and whose influence made me the woman I am today. She was my best friend, my compass, the better part of what it means to be a mom, a lady and, above all things, human. She was *the* strongest woman I knew, and she was dying.

As Hope's only daughter, I had no idea how to stand back and let that happen, and so I did the only thing I could do. I put my faith in God, and I kept a dying woman's wish. In doing so, I unearthed an epic love story, the one I've been holding out for my whole life. It turned out to be so much more than I could have ever dreamed. For a kid who was voted "Biggest Dreamer" by her middle school homeroom class, that's saying something.

Growing up, I was never one to give in easily. I was stubborn, as willful and as resourceful as they come. From an early age I was determined to push the envelope—be my own girl. When I was just two years old, Mom invited our neighbor over for lunch,

a woman and her young daughter who lived down the street. Always happy for the chance to doll her little girl up, Mom wrestled me into a frilly dress, patent leather shoes and pigtails pulled so tight, my head still aches. Midway through lunch, not only did I sneak into the backyard, tear off my dress, shoes and under bits, but I convinced our neighbor's daughter into doing the same.

I've always been pretty persuasive.

The two of us were caught running amok (naked!) in the backyard. The garden hose was also running, and our pretty party dresses were in a sopping heap. I'm pretty sure there's an incriminating photograph of it somewhere.

That determined little girl developed into a ten-year-old tomboy who fell in love with love and basketball. From the third grade to the fifth, I was the only girl to play on a YMCA boys' basketball team. Mom always encouraged me to be fiercely independent and brave, until the day she died. Yet, somehow, that didn't keep her from relentlessly picking apart my life choices. The older I got, the more we butted heads, particularly when it came to fashion and romance. I was stubborn in my ways, even more than she was, which often drove her crazy.

Some days, it was all she could do to keep from bursting a blood vessel. She'd say, "If I had your big, green eyes, I would walk out the door every day looking like Liz Taylor."

To which I would reply, "And if I used *that* much eye shadow and mascara, I'd still be rolling my eyes at you, only looking like Cleopatra."

This cosmetic commentary coming from the woman who, as a teenager, seriously considered becoming a nun. I could always be counted on to remind her that I had seen photographs of her when she was young. Mom had big, beautiful, almond-shaped, brown eyes, and except for a little mascara, she did not wear makeup. She didn't have to. Her olive-toned skin was flawless. It wasn't until she started dating my dad that she started dabbling in women's war paint. Mom's motto: A woman has got to suffer to be beautiful.

She told me that when she and my dad were first married, she would wait for him to fall asleep before putting rollers in her hair. Then she would sneak out of bed in the morning, long before the sun was up, and take them out. I can just see her teasing and backcombing her hair before the light of day and then crawling back into bed looking like Jackie Onassis. I suppose Dad was in love with her enough to believe that she rolled out of bed looking like that.

God love him.

Mom was a natural beauty, but what made her particularly pretty was that she had a good and grateful heart. It showed in everything she did. She was the one who raised my brother and me to be good to others. She'd pack us up into the car, along with big boxes of gently-worn clothes and toys, all the stuff we had outgrown, and we'd drive around dilapidated neighborhoods looking for a good home. I remember her stopping in front of a small, white house with a handful of children playing in the front yard. The paint was chipped. The lawn was mostly dirt. She knocked on the front door and asked the young mother if she could use a big box of children's clothing and toys. The woman broke into tears, giving my mother the best hug. I could feel it from the backseat of the car. I was young, but that made an impression on me.

Except for Mom's early morning curler regime and her love of black coffee, I am a lot like her, more than I care to admit sometimes. And, in my bleak defense, it wasn't like I didn't like to wear makeup. I did.

I do!

I just don't like to cake it on. Even in her last days at Hospice, while the nurse was in the middle of changing her bedsheets with her still in bed, Mom needled me about it. Through squinty, brown eyes, she looked at me and said, "You need lipstick."

"*Really*, Mom?"

"Did you put on *any* makeup today?"

"As a matter of fact, I did," I declared.

"It doesn't look like it."

"Oh my god!" I said, rifling through my bag and grabbing a tube of Burt's Bees—fig flavor. She watched as I smeared some on.

"Happy?"

"I can't tell. It's too light," she replied.

Okay, so Burt's Bees isn't *really* lipstick, but at least it afforded my face some hint of color. The truth was, I wasn't wearing much makeup that afternoon because of the good cry I had on the ride over. I was feeling a bit beat up, having substituted for high school freshman all day. Most of the time, I had the endurance for teenage angst, but because I was days away from losing Mom, the chink in my armor left me wide open to the mother of all high school mean girls. She must have smelled blood in the water because, over the course of one class period, she came at me with teeth bared.

Truth be told, I was feeling sorry for myself in those last few weeks, not to mention exhausted. In all fairness, I was facing the same reality most Disney characters face—being motherless. I cried when Bambi lost his mother, and (Yeah!) I cried at the thought of losing mine. Hence, no makeup. It got washed away in the flood of tears and snot on the way over. I didn't say anything to Mom about it. The spigot was still a little leaky, and I didn't want to risk another break. Giving me that look only moms can give, she said, "You have your dad's lips. Lipstick helps."

"Yes, mother."

What she meant was, without lipstick, I don't have lips. The nurse smiled and winked at me, as she finished making up

Mom's bed. It's funny, Mom has been gone for four years now, and *these* are the stories that stick. Having been named for Natalie Wood (Dad's Hollywood crush), and occasionally compared to Elizabeth Taylor, I had a lot to live up to—cosmetically speaking. Add to that the task of being Hope's daughter. Well, let's just say I don't travel too far without a tube of lipstick at the ready—or my version of it anyway. That's the thing about a mother's influence. Good, bad or ugly, it stays with you—forever!

Mom's name was Esperanza. That's Spanish for Hope. It was fitting because Mom was that and so much more to her children and grandchildren. She was a petite Hispanic woman who, thanks to Paul Newman, was a sucker for blue eyes. I'm convinced that's the reason she married my dad—a tall, blonde, blue-eyed gringo whose ancestors, I'm told, crossed over on a ship from Switzerland.

Blue eyes were her kryptonite.

Mom didn't say much, but when she did, it would behoove you to listen. Most of the time when I was rolling my eyes at her, and not just as a teenager, it was because I was genuinely annoyed by the fact that she was usually right. Nevertheless, as her only daughter, I did my level best to rebel, right up until the very end. What I failed to recognize was that the better part of Mom's influence came to me honestly. That is to say, I am the woman I am today *because* of her example. It didn't matter how much I resisted.

Oscar Wilde said it best, "*All women become like their mothers. That is their tragedy. No man does. That's his.*"

The man knew what he was talking about.

One of the key impacts Mom had on my life was talking me into a job at American Express. Now, there was a professional rabbit hole. However, because she worked there and because I didn't have an "action plan" after graduating high school, she twisted my arm. I'll admit, while it wasn't what I imagined myself doing, the gig was good in that it set me up with a steady paycheck, great benefits, job experience, college reimbursement and a cool, new car—a 1986 Chevrolet Camaro with vanity plates that read: SHZBAD. I was, of course, referencing the 80s Keith Sweat song that was hot at the time.

It wasn't bad for a nineteen-year-old starting out at the bottom rung of Corporate America. While working as a clerk, one step below a secretary, wasn't my schtick, per se, I committed to it for one year, thinking my dream job of becoming a New York Times best-selling author was just around the corner.

Nineteen years later.

I woke up in public relations as a communication specialist, in the bowels of the American Express building. I was divorced with two little boys, having spent the better part of my life and career at a Fortune 100 company at a time when women wore panty hose and men wore neckties to the office. I miss men in neckties, but not so much the panty hose.

My corporate career was like a good marriage. It provided

an excellent education in professionalism, lots of opportunity for growth, and I had no less than eight weeks of vacation every year, not to mention tons of sick time. That's a blessing for a single mom. Still, the work never quite turned me on if you know what I mean. Even though I had worked my way up to a job that paid *really* well, allowing me to walk around with a five-thousand-dollar camera strung around my neck and the ability to write, albeit corporate communications, I was still the starry-eyed idealist. I was hopelessly dotting my i's with hearts on interoffice envelopes and purchase orders, despite my boss' request not to do so.

I was Peter Parker in a pencil skirt!

I daydreamed of doing *anything* else for a living, preferably something more creative, inspiring and gratifying. In the meantime, I managed to get two college degrees and, as far as feeling gratified in my work, I was getting warmer. I was good at the people part, just not the politics. I lacked the killer instinct.

After almost twenty years of being polished in the corporate world, I still refused to color inside the lines. I was never one to fully accede to the world's demands, so I found creative ways to insert my ownness into my corporate workload, if not the world at large. It got me through to 2008 when I was mercifully laid off with 7,000 other American Express employees.

When our leadership team flew out from New York to deliver the news, one employee at a time, I think they were surprised by the giant grin on my face. Most everyone else took advantage of the big box of Kleenex on the boardroom table, breaking down into tears, but I was much more optimistic. I was looking forward to my one year's severance, so that I might change the trajectory of my course … and my life. I saw it as a gift, along with the words Mom left me with that morning. Knowing I was about to get the boot, she said, "They can't eat you, Nat."

It's been thirteen years since American Express laid me off, and I am *still* that optimistic girl, only now I am a grandmother of two little boys, Eli and Asher, and I keep my clothes on at parties. I still dot my i's with hearts, only now I do it on Love Notes to our nation's heroes, those who deserve more love than they get these days.

Suffice it to say, I found my purpose— my ownness in a mission (i.e., movement) that Mom and I started together at the worst possible time. This

errand I am on is just me, a stubborn woman who is in love with love, randomly delivering handwritten hope to a world that is not accustomed to receiving it, not without the expectation of giving something in return. I know not everyone gets that about me or this mission, but it's all good. I'm used to people looking at me cockeyed. That's how I know I'm on the right track. As *the* biggest dreamer in the room, bewildered gazes are my business.

Once I make up my mind about a thing, I go headlong into

it, no matter what anyone thinks, says, or expects. If you don't believe me, ask the mama goat that once wandered onto the farm I grew up on. If goats could talk, she would tell you of my persistence, even at five years old. She wasn't our goat. I'm not exactly sure who she belonged to. Nevertheless, I set out to catch and milk her one day. I was a farm girl. That's what farm girls do! We milk things—for all they're worth.

With nothing more than a smile and a yard of twine, I lured her in, lassoed her and squeezed milk from her teats into a rusted soup can that I found in the dirt behind the chicken coop. I filled the can half full, as would any self-respecting optimist, and even though Mom told me we couldn't drink the milk, I remember feeling quite good about myself. I can't say as much for the goat.

Since that day, Mom nicknamed me "Gluey," as in I stick to stuff. Not much has changed since then. I am still a dreamer, a stick-to-it do-gooder who, at the risk of sounding a lot like a Tom Petty song, "loves her mama and America, too." I am an old-fashioned girl who believes the best in people, the glass-half-full kind of girl. Call me naïve, but I have always given people the benefit of the doubt, and it has served me well.

Have I been let down?

Of course.

Has it caused me to lose faith in folks?

No.

I guess I am stubborn that way, too.

Super gluey.

Hence, here I am at the most compelling chapter of my life. And it all began on the heels of a broken heart. It was a simple Love Note, a handwritten gesture of gratitude that changed everything. A life of stationery was my destiny, not a stationary life, and everything I ever dreamed for was just outside of my comfort zone.

No goats were harmed in the making of this book.

Natalie, we all have flaws and a purpose in life. Some have hearts that are bigger than the rest of us. In my humble opinion, that is you. You and your mom have started something that makes those of us on the sidelines realize how much of an impact we can make on those who serve selflessly to keep us safe. Love what you do!

—Robin B.

ONE
Glimmer of Hope

I was sitting pretzel-style on my couch, staring at a blank, white wall on Valentine's Day. My stomach was tied in knots. It was 2016, a mere five months after Mom's incurable cancer diagnosis—multiple myeloma. We were told by her oncologist, a medical professional who was about as warm and fuzzy as a metal speculum used in a woman's pap smear, devoid of human warmth and dignity, that with on-going treatment, the disease could be managed for years. While it wasn't what we were hoping for, we weren't without hope.

A few months into chemotherapy, Mom was ready to throw in the towel. It was awful. On the mornings of her weekly treatment, she would wake up sick to her stomach. Every trip to the doctor was an ordeal. I can't tell you how unnerving this was for me, her only daughter turned primary caregiver. She had always been my rock, the one I leaned on and looked up to my whole life, all five foot nothing of her. Suddenly she was frail and fearful, not nearly the pillar of strength I knew her to be. On top of which, our roles had reversed. I didn't know what to do with that, and there were days I resented her for it. Selfishly, I could take anybody's frailty but hers.

Nine times out of ten, Mom's oncologist, a tall, lanky man of middle-eastern decent, who I shall refer to as "Dr. Duck Lips" for his cold, speculum-like bedside manner, would end her appointments by standing up and walking out of the exam room whilst speaking into a handheld, digital voice recorder. He would leave without so much as a "So long" or "See you later." Mom and I would be left sitting there, wringing our hands, until one of us would finally ask, "Are we done?"

Dr. Duck Lips wasn't convinced that Mom's adverse reaction to the chemotherapy wasn't psychosomatic. He even went so far as to say that because the dosage was so light, she shouldn't have *any* negative side effects—none, whatsoever. Sometimes he would even snicker and debate with her when she'd go into detail about the severe symptoms she was experiencing, including nausea, diarrhea, loss of appetite, exhaustion and depression. A part of me hated him for coming off so smug, but there was a small part of me that wanted to agree with him and even used that medical intelligence against her, as a means to get her to her next appointment.

"Your doctor says you should not be getting *this* sick," I'd say, as she'd press a big, wadded-up beach towel to her mouth, dry heaving all the way to her chemo appointment.

As much as I wanted to believe Mom's symptoms were psychosomatic, the yellow bile on the floorboard of my Jeep did not lie. Whether it was all in her head or not, Mom was sick, and she was, indeed, dying. She didn't lose her hair, but she did lose her will, along with a lot of weight, mostly because she was tossing her cookies at the mere mention of the word cancer, not that she was eating—mind you. It got so bad, I started storing makeshift barf bags in the backseat, anything to keep that god-awful stench of foamy bile contained.

I felt like the bad guy, the evil villain twisting her arm all the way to and from those dreadful appointments. My younger brother offered to help, but she refused him. She didn't want her "baby" to see her like that. She wanted to protect him. I know it sounds petty, but I resented it. As the dutiful daughter and big sister, I took exception to the fact that the role of caregiver fell primarily on my shoulders, and that resentment only fed my growing guilt. It was an ugly cycle, which is probably why I went into survival mode, not allowing myself to feel anything more than determined.

It was all I could do to get through the day and to get Mom to her appointments. I wanted to be anywhere, but where I was—a terminally-single, empty nester sitting alone in my living room, playing hostess to Camille on Valentine's Day. While my Facebook friends were sitting fireside with their families on camping trips, posing for photos with brand-new grandbabies in their laps, enjoying steak dinners at fancy restaurants, and fussing over bouquets of flowers and boxes of chocolates, I was alone in my living room, feeling so damn sorry for myself I could barely breathe.

It was awful.

Mom's cancer, and her need to keep it just between us, was slowly eating away at me, dashing any hopes I may have had for the next big chapter in my life. I'm not proud of it, but I was the poster girl for pessimism, which is not characteristic of me, not even in the worst of times. However, this was different. I didn't know what to do with the unconstructive thoughts and feelings I was having, so I kept them to myself, which only made matters worse. The littlest things tried my patience, like when Mom would affix apple stickers onto the gooseneck of my kitchen faucet after washing her fruit. Rather than being happy that she was (finally!) eating, I was irked that she couldn't throw those things away. I found myself mumbling under my breath every time I saw one or two of those silly things adorning my kitchen sink.

Ridiculous, I know.

At the time, I had just gotten my brood up and out of the nest with very little incident. My boys, Billy and Alec, grew into good, strong, healthy, educated men. As for me, my career was in a bit of a slump. I was working for peanuts at Arizona State University, a desk jockey who landed a magnificent corner office with nowhere to go from there. And as for romance, it was a myth, something I only read about in books.

In the fifteen years I had been divorced, I had one serious relationship. That is, if you can count a long-distance relationship as being "serious," considering my love interest and I were both single parents at the time, living 2,613 miles apart—a stone's throw from hopeless. He was a mountain man, a writer/home inspector living in the woods of Princeton, Massachusetts. He drove a Jeep Wrangler and sang old, sea shanties to me on an acoustic guitar. The man chopped his own firewood, which means I may have only been in love with the idea of him. It lasted just shy of one year.

Surprise.

Nevertheless, the breakup took its toll on me, putting me off men for a while. However, on the upside, it got me into a size six slacks. Looking back, the one man I could always count on for anything was my ex-husband. We were unable to make our marriage work, but somehow, we managed a relatively happy split. Save a few squabbles, it was a dream divorce. At the boys' ballgames and school recitals, most people didn't even know that he and I were no longer married. We got along well because, at the end of the day, we were both bonkers about our boys. To this day, he and I end nearly every conversation with the words, "I love you."

And we mean it.

Having my ex-husband in my life is probably one of the reasons I stayed single for so long. In many ways, I still had a "man" to take care of those things that men are good at taking care of, like oil changes and water-heater repairs.

You thought I was going to say sex, right?!

Yeah ... no. In that department, I'll admit, life got a little lonely in the boudoir, but rather than search high and low for a good man, I doubled my efforts in raising two of them. I became a football mom, corner-house soup kitchen for my boys and their buddies. On top of which, I went back to school to finish my second degree. I became a columnist for the local paper. I traveled as much as I could with my kids. Life got pretty hectic, and when life got heavy, the Hallmark Channel helped—a lot!

It wasn't until I reached the great sandwich generation that

I realized I might have missed my window of opportunity, romantically speaking. I was sitting there, stuck somewhere in the middle of caring for my dying mother and letting go of my children. It was a rough (ROUGH!) patch. All the major players in my life had been given their marching papers. They were all on their way out, in one way or another—college, military, terminal illness. Even my ex-husband had proposed marriage to his long-term girlfriend. And there I was, the pitiful one left holding the bag. I had never felt more alone.

I remember one Christmas Eve, in particular. I was down with a miserable cold. Mom was visiting my brother and his family. My boys were at their dad's house, and I was home alone, stuck on the couch, nursing ginger ale and saltine crackers, watching Casablanca, looking (and feeling!) a lot like roadkill. My ex called that evening and insisted I get cleaned up and come eat prime rib with them—the boys, the girlfriend and her parents. While it was a pity invite, I appreciated it because, of all my friends and family, he was the *only* one to reach out. And he wouldn't take no for an answer. Reluctantly, I accepted. I mustered a shower and then put on the fanciest pair of sweats I owned. I drove two miles down the road to his place and sat down to dinner with good people. As nice as it was, I still felt like the odd man out.

Suddenly, being single wasn't a choice. I was on the hook, which left little time, energy, and freedom for love, let alone sex and male companionship. With Mom living a short distance down the hall from me, sex was off the table or off any piece of furniture for that matter. It was no wonder I was feeling sorry for myself. It had been a dog's year since I had laid down with a man, much less been kissed by one. I'm talking *really* kissed—Clark Gable soldiering up to fight a war in the South, taking-his-woman-in-his-arms-and-planting-one-on-her kind of kiss. It was a horrifying realization, especially for a romantic, like me. Even worse, was managing this load all by myself. My brother had his wife. My ex had his fiancé. My boys had their lives, and I had two tuxedo cats who seemed perfectly indifferent to all of my drama. Thank God for my bathtub. It was my only solace.

I was following in Mom's footsteps—flying solo, destined for a life unaccompanied. The one thing she had that I did not … a daughter to take care of her when it counted.

When Mom divorced my dad, Mom purposefully chose to stay single, the way in which a vegan purposefully chooses to delete dairy from their diet—for their own good. She honestly believed there was only one true love in every woman's life, which was fine for her, but I didn't believe that.

What self-respecting hopeless romantic would?

I was hopeful in finding love again. So, I prayed for it. I believed for it. I held out for it. I even asked out loud for it, in the same way I asked for the paperclip.

My kingdom for a good man!

However, on *that* day, Valentine's Day 2016, I was ready to resign to a "vegan" lifestyle when it came to love. As Mom became more willful, demanding and sick, a part of me felt like I, too, was terminal—terminally single and on my own. On top of which, she was literally pushing people away. Having become so dependent on me, she was resisting the help of anyone else. She wanted *me* to do all the heavy lifting, and the more she pushed for it, the more resigned I became.

"I don't want your brother to see me like this," she insisted, when I suggested recruiting his help. "Besides, he has a life!"

Ouch! No four words had ever hurt so much.

Mind you, I was merely suggesting my brother drive her to doctor appointments every other week. I wasn't about to subject him to all the other stuff that goes with chemotherapy and a terminal illness. I just needed a breather. I needed my brother. The whole thing was wearing on me, and, so, in a huff I exclaimed, "That's not fair. I *need* his help, and he *wants* to help."

"No," she demanded, digging in her heels.

Mom fought me on it, tooth and nail, but in the end, I made the executive decision to call for back up because 1.) I was bigger than she was, and 2.) My brother was only too happy to drive her to doctor appointments. Even though they lived on the opposite end of town, no less than sixty miles away, my brother and his wife wanted to contribute to her care, and it made a tremendous difference, not only to me but to everyone involved, including Mom.

This was hard for her. I got that. It was hard for us all. The path of the dying is never an easy one. The one thing that brought me peace in my persistence is that Mom never gave up on those she loved—*ever*! And, so, while I wonder if there were days that I pushed her too hard or expected too much, there is a part of me that knows she would have done the same for me. After all, I am my mother's daughter.

Just before she fell ill, Mom retired as a paraprofessional at a local high school. When it came to helping students succeed in school, she was a fierce advocate. She loved teaching, and even though she wasn't a certified teacher, per se, she was, indeed, an educator at heart. And despite having never graduated with a four-year degree, she did receive and strongly encouraged a college education. She advocated for it, to none more than her children and grandchildren.

"I want all of mine to be college graduates," she'd implore. "I want *that* to be my legacy."

So far, so good, Mom!

Hope had a soft spot for teenagers. She genuinely felt for them. I think that's why her students loved her so much. She understood them. She talked with them, helped them with their schoolwork and struggles. She did so without falling prey to their antics. Take it from somebody who knows, the woman was great at calling your bluff, which, at the end of the day, her students appreciated. They were better for it.

We all were.

Deep down, Mom believed that people want (and need!)

someone to love them and to believe in them enough to be forthright and to have expectations of them. She would often say, "If no one expects anything of you, it's as if no one cares enough about what happens to you. That can be damaging."

I got the feeling she was speaking from experience. *That* was when I realized that Mom was not behaving like the woman she raised me to be. If our roles had been reversed, had I been the one diagnosed with a terminal illness, flat-out refusing to get out of bed, she never would have allowed it—not for one minute. She would have *expected* that I keep pushing forward as best I could. That was the glimmer of Hope I needed, that still, small voice inside of me that turned our adversity on its ear. In life, our presence is our superpower. And, at that point, neither Mom nor I was very present. Just being there was not enough. We had to get out and *do* something to make a positive impact, lest we regret the things we did not do. It was suddenly all so clear.

Hello ... I just want to tell you a story about my mom. You see, she was out at a Baskin-Robbin's on Saturday night, February 20th, celebrating my dad's birthday, driving my dad's car, which has veteran plates. When she came out, there was a small card tucked under her wiper with some very sweet words. The part of the story you don't know is that my dad passed away a little over three years ago, just shy of his 60th birthday and their 40th wedding anniversary. Baskin-Robbin's was his first job when he was in high school in Northern California, and it was always his favorite— pistachio ice cream, to be exact. He and my mom are both veterans. They had three daughters, and mostly due to the military, we are scattered across the country. My husband and I are also veterans and hanging out in northern California. One sister is in Montana with a brand-new baby boy, all by herself, while her husband is deployed and the other is in Indiana, chasing her horsey dreams. And we all were doing something on Saturday to remember our dad/husband. So, you see, that one little note that took a handful of minutes to write didn't just bring a small smile to one person. It brought tears that rippled across the country. So, thank you.

—Mischa W., Military Veteran

TWO
Call to Adventure

I t was time to take a good, hard and honest look at myself. The moment of truth is never easy. It means looking yourself (and life) in the eye and doing what is necessary to endure, no matter how difficult the road ahead. Within every hero's journey, this is what is known as the "Call to Adventure," a launching point for the plucky protagonist to face her dragon, lest it consume her. This was my dragon, my watershed moment. I would have given anything to hear Mom's (unsolicited) two cents that day, but as I peeked into her bedroom, I got nothing but an empty gaze. I was already at a loss, and she wasn't even gone. Her sudden apathy toward me and life, in general, wrecked me. Had she been her usual, clever self, she would have given me those squinty, brown eyes and said something to the effect of, "All is well, Nat!"

From her lips to God's ears.

Most days, that small vote of confidence was all I needed to get my act together. The more I thought about it, the more I realized it was *that* brand of love, the kind dispensed in a handful of stirring words, that moves people. Who among us couldn't use that on any given day? Mom was that for me. She was my voice of reason, wise deliberate and inordinately intuitive. She always had a calming, confidence-building effect on me. At the same time, she had her own misgivings, stuff that held her back.

Mom was quiet, reserved and bashful around people she didn't know, to the point of being meek. As her daughter, it was always surprising to see that side of her. She always said that people misread her quietness for shyness, and that her diffident disposition had more to do with a speech impediment she had as a child than anything else. When she was little, Mom loved to sing. Her elders would prop her up on tabletops for her to perform, and because of a childhood lisp, they laughed and teased her. So, she stopped talking altogether. Perhaps that was the reason Mom grew into a woman of few words, not to mention intent on raising confident kids.

Before cancer, she always knew the right thing to say. She was quick, witty and could deliver comebacks like nobody's business. She was also the one person (outside of my youngest son) to nudge me, embolden me and push me to act when circumstance called for it. However, since she was further down in the dumps than I was that day, thanks to a terminal diagnosis and a debilitating treatment, I needed to be the one to pull us out of this devasting nosedive. I wondered, *What would Mom say?*

My eyes welled with tears. I was literally at the end of my rope when the words came to me, *"They can't eat you, Nat."*

Okay. So, life tripped us up. And, yes, it hurts—a lot! While there is no harm in laying low for a little while, at some point, a girl has got to get up off her tush and do what warriors do—battle!

Lest she spend the rest of her life nursing regret. But let's be honest. It takes a lot more than poetic platitudes to take sword in hand and run into the fray, and no amount of romanticizing is going to dress up a gal's war wounds or make surviving them any easier.

We've all experienced a broken heart, but a girl has got to do herself a favor and make nice with her pain. Listen to it, but don't turn down the sheets for it or leave a chocolate on its pillow. Sit with it, but don't allow it to get too comfortable. Pain has its purpose. Its job is simply to make you aware that something is wrong. It was never meant to stick around, so thank it and kindly, albeit firmly, ask it to leave. Easier said than done—I know. But ask yourself this question: Will your pain leave its mark on the world, or will you?

"Get dressed, and meet me at the kitchen table," I said, my hands pressed firmly on my hips. "It's Valentine's Day."

For the first time in weeks, Mom looked me in the eye. It was as if she had been waiting for me to take a hard stance. In the small flutter of her feet, as she kicked off the covers and rolled out of bed, just as I had done thousands of times when she'd wake me for school, the idea for Love Notes was born.

We didn't have a whole lot to work with. What we did have was a little imagination, card stock and some ink. Mom and I bellied up to the pub-style kitchen table. I threw a few boxes of blank thank-you cards in the middle, and we got to work. Mom suggested we focus our efforts on our nation's veterans and first responders.

"They need lots of love," she said.

Mom felt for those who served our country and our community, partly because her first grandson, Billy, had served in the US Navy. And partly  because he was about to serve as a police officer in the state of Georgia. On top of which, her uncles, Martin and Gabriel Tafoya, served in the US Army. I was told they left their hometown of Cubero, New Mexico on March 20, 1941, so to join the 200 Coast Artillery Division. Martin was thirty years old, and Gabriel was just twenty-two when they went missing during the Bataan Death March in 1942. They were among the 36,000 troops serving under Major General Edward P. King, Jr. when they surrendered to the Japanese.

Prisoners of war, they were forced to walk eighty-five miles in just twelve days to prison camps in the northern territory. On the day they arrived at the destination, the Japanese came for one brother, and the very next day they came for the other. Martin and Gabriel were never seen again. Their bodies were never recovered. Mom's eyes watered when she shared how her grandmother, Martin and Gabriel's mother, could be heard for miles, wailing from a nearby peak. Her pleas echoed through the canyon, "Where are my boys? Did the Japanese eat them?"

It was on the heels of that story that Mom put pen to paper. It was the first real spark I had seen from her in months. That Valentine's Day, we set out on a journey of writing fifty Love Notes, predominantly for veterans. We wrote a small handful of Valentines for first responders and everyday humans, as well. But the real push, in that moment, was for our nation's military heroes.

After two hours, and as many homemade Reuben sandwiches, I bundled Mom up and got her into my Jeep. Over the next three hours, we set out on a mission to find our heroes. We left Love Notes on the windshields of their cars. We hand delivered a few to war veterans in the grocery store and to a police officer pumping gas. It opened the door to conversation, inviting us into these people's stories. By the time we returned home, having delivered almost all fifty Love Notes, we were laughing so hard that our smiles hurt. I'll never forget Mom leaning over and saying, "I can't remember why I was so worried."

From that day forward, we got up every morning with a sense of purpose. We faithfully wrote handfuls of Love Notes at our local coffee shop. We carried those notes of gratitude in our purses, close to our hearts. We handed them out every chance we got. Some days, we'd get in the car and spend hours driving around looking for these heroes. What began as a means of self-preservation became so much more. The experience, itself, transformed us.

Little did we know that we were rebounding into something bigger than the both of us. If it hadn't been for that small hour of desperation and the act of handwriting a Love Note, I don't know how I would have survived this woman. For months I had  been praying for a hero, for someone to swoop in and save the day. Turned out, Mom was, too.

A few months later, as I was kneeling next to the tub, bathing her and washing her hair, Mom looked up at me with child-like eyes and said, "Who knew that when I was bathing my baby girl in a little plastic tub all those years ago, she would turn around and do the same for me one day? I gave birth to my hero."

My heart caught in my throat. Salty tears stung my eyes. I had no idea how to respond to that. I was nobody's hero. The truth was I was scared to death most days, operating in survival mode, focusing on the things I could control, like getting Mom to her doctor appointments, keeping her comfortable and pouring her into Epsom-salt baths. The simple tasks of washing her hair, rubbing her down with lavender lotion, keeping her in fuzzy socks and fresh pajamas with an endless supply of fudgsicles—some of her favorite things—is what kept me on course.

For two years, I did everything in my power to make her stay in my guestroom warm, cozy and want of nothing. Truth: I spoiled her rotten—in princess proportions. I gave her what she gave me growing up, the comfort and security of a mother's love. And like any mother worth her salt, I never let on that I, myself, was scared shitless. That little tidbit I kept between me and God. I also kept my faith and my favorite bible verse within reach—Matthew (17:20). Surmise to say, all a girl really needs to thrive is "faith the size of a mustard seed."

The reason for my email is to try and explain how much your card and your words meant to me. It broke my heart! I'm not a touchy-feely type. In fact, I am about as far opposite from that as you can imagine. I owned a karate school for years, worked as a cop and now I do executive protection (bodyguard) work. But your card touched a part of my heart that has laid dormant for longer than I can imagine. You touched a sacred part of my soul with your kind words and compassion. You brought tears to my eyes, and I had to stop my car. I doubt you can imagine how much your card and your beautiful handwriting meant to me. Thank you. THANK YOU from the purest part of my spirit! May God bless you for your kindness, compassion and your selfless spirit!

—Larry W., USMC Grunt

THREE

The Springboard

S ince I was a little girl, I always dreamed for a life less ordinary. I have always believed in the magic of miracles. I always felt like there were big things in store for me. Believing in such things is, in my opinion, half the battle. The other half is realizing that *you*, yourself, are the magic and the miracle.

From what I can tell, at the end of life, it has little relevance how much power and position you hold, let alone fame and fortune. None of that stuff amounts to a hill of beans, unless you use it for good. What will have mattered is having used up your God-given gifts, giving them away freely to others, whether you think they deserve it or not. In giving the best of yourself, no matter how much or how little you have, you get the best of others in return, oftentimes from people you never would have dreamed.

For me, my gift is my pen. When I realized the punch that was packed in my Ballpoint and in a single handwritten Love Note, I knew that Mom and I were onto something special and that delivering handwritten words of encouragement was *the* thing that would separate an ordinary life from an extraordinary one. It was something I unwittingly experimented with twenty-two years earlier, not long after my divorce. It was such a simple, yet powerful act, writing love notes on paper napkins and tucking them into my firstborn son's sack lunch every morning. This artless gesture took a scared, little boy and made him brave.

Billy was seven years old. He was in the third grade, and while he wore a brave smile, I knew he was having a tough time in school. His dad and I were going through a divorce, albeit relatively amicable. Billy and his little brother, Alec, were starting the year off at a brand-new school, in a brand-new neighborhood, in a brand-new house. Our life was being rebuilt from the ground up. Nothing about it felt familiar. We were all fumbling to find our feet.

Billy's biggest worry was that he was losing his dad in this new deal. It was up to me to convince him otherwise and to reassure him that everything was going to be okay. So, every morning, to bolster Billy's bravery, I would scribble a love note on a plain, white paper napkin. I would fill each note up with meaningful words of encouragement to help get him through the day, confidence-building words like, "*Billy is so brave!*" I signed each one, "*Love, Mom.*" Those love notes became our thing, his and mine, and more often than not, they would make their way back home to me at the end of the school day. I would find them crumpled up in Billy's pants pockets or at the bottom of his backpack. Not once, throughout the entire third grade, did he throw away my love notes. In fact, there were days he would reply to them with love notes of his own. On one note, he wrote back to me in black Sharpie. The words were smudged by his tears. It read: "Mom, I love you, and you love me. That's the way it will always be."

I still have that one.

I didn't think much of it until one day, several years down the road. I was cleaning out Billy's backpack on the last day of his junior year in high school. Deep in the side pocket, I found a heaping handful of plain, white paper napkins, the same kind of napkins I had been packing in his sack lunch for years, only without the handwriting. I stopped that gesture in the fourth grade, even though I was still packing his lunch all the way through high school.

"Billy, why in the world are you holding onto these things?" I asked, counting no less than twenty clean napkins. Billy looked at me with those big, green eyes of his and said, "Because they remind me of you, Mom. I didn't have the heart to throw them away."

Gulp.

Those little love notes I wrote for Billy still had a shelf life, and even though I hadn't actually written one in years, the memory of them held fast to his heart. That scared, little boy grew up to be a hunky linebacker on the varsity football team, a deployed sailor for the United States Navy, a police officer in the state of Georgia, and now a big, strong sheriff's deputy in the state of Texas. I like to think my Love Notes had a little something to do with that. Billy is, indeed, brave, which goes to show the power of the pen and the words used to encourage, if not move others to be and do their best.

People will either shrink or expand to meet others' expectations of them—good, bad or indifferent. *That*, in a nutshell, was the "big idea," the springboard behind the Nothing but Love Notes movement. What began as a means to an end turned out to be the happy ending. I didn't even see it coming, although I did get a fortune cookie not long before it all began. It read: "*You will be recognized and honored as a community leader.*"

Ah, the power of positive thinking!

Ma'am, I have to be quite honest with you. I was pretty upset to see something getting put on my window. When I read your note, I almost broke into tears. The only thing I could think of was to chase you down and give you a hug, a small token of my appreciation and gratitude for you. Although you may not know it, your notes and your thoughtfulness do not go unnoticed. I cannot tell you what that meant to me to read that, as I am sure there are many more veterans that feel the same as me. Thank you for starting my week off this way, as it will be a very difficult one. Thank you for making a stranger feel like there are still good people and that the job we did was not in vain. From the bottom of my heart, THANK YOU!!!!

—— Jeremiah T., U.S. Army Veteran (Your parking lot hug)

FOUR
Parking Lot Hug

My purpose was handed to me in the shape of an envelope, a simple, paper container with a sealable flap that holds a little handwritten hope for our everyday heroes. Throughout my life, Mom was always my hope, my hero, so, it's no surprise that I find myself in the "business" of delivering hope.

God knows the world needs it.

If you ask me, nobody needs and deserves hope more than the everyday American hero, the run-into-the-fire-and-fray, take-a-bullet-for-you un-caped crusader who is overworked, underpaid, and least appreciated. That said, it is our first responders and military veterans who often take exception to being called a "hero." I know this because my Love Notes are often met with the obligatory, "Just doing my job, Ma'am."

God love them for it.

I suppose that is why I do what I do. I have seen the toll their work takes—the blood, the sweat, and the tears. I am inspired to love on these men and women even more because of it—despite their humble protest. These heroes are not looking for a pat on the back. They're just "doing their job," and who else would do what they do? You? Me?

When I hand a Love Note to our nation's best and bravest, they are often thrown off guard, which makes me sort of sad that this brand of love doesn't happen more often. It also makes me kind of happy because I love delivering the unexpected! That's where the magic is, and the subsequent joy of giving.

In every interaction I have with a Love Note recipient, there is a minor miracle involved. Like I said, people don't expect to receive random kindnesses from a stranger, not without requiring something in return. As one of my favorite firefighters (Ryan!) put it, "it's not characteristic of our society," which sort of makes Nothing but Love Notes a glitch in the system—an anomaly.

Now, that gives me a heart-on!

One hot, summer afternoon in June 2016, I got a small whiff of my superpower. I was walking out of the grocery store when I noticed a big, white truck parked up front in the handicap zone. The veteran license plate gave this particular hero away.

With two grocery bags dangling from my wrist, filled to the brim with the makings of a summer salad, enough produce to choke a horse, I clumsily rifled through my purse for a veteran Love Note. I was in a bit of a hurry, so I didn't notice the veteran and his pregnant wife, Macy, standing next to the truck. After surreptitiously tucking the note underneath the windshield wiper, I turned to walk away. That's when I heard a salty, gruff (Read: Angry!) voice exclaim, "What the f*@% did she put on my truck?"

Oh. My. God!

The hair on the back of my neck stood up. I didn't bother looking back. With the handles of the heavy plastic bags cutting into my wrist and the leafy tops from the fresh celery stalks flopping wildly about, nearly becoming a casualty in the chase, I darted back to my car where Mom, my aunt and my cousin were waiting for me. I was just four months into this little mission, and nothing like that had ever happened before. Heck, in all my life, nothing like that had ever happened before. By the time I got to the car, me *and* the ingredients for the summer salad had been thoroughly tossed.

As I chucked that night's chow into the trunk, I looked up to see a man (the salty veteran!) running at me. He was a mountain of a man, all neck, pecks, and shoulders—Stretch Armstrong in a tank top and blue jeans. Like a deer in the headlights, I froze. I had no idea what was about to happen. There was no time to flee or to pee or to pass out. The only thing I had time to do was brace for impact. Thrusting the car key between my forefinger and middle finger, just as I was taught in self-defense class, I took a warrior stance, albeit a bit wobbly. As the young veteran buttonholed me in the back forty, I noticed his blue eyes were wet and his expression wilted, not at all what I was expecting to see after detonating a proverbial tripwire of profanities that could be heard two zip codes away.

"Thank you," he whispered, holding the Love Note up and

clearing a rather large frog from his throat. "You caught me on a *really* rotten day. I needed this."

Speechless, my lips curled up into a shaky smile.

"Can I hug you," he asked.

I nodded, and the next thing I knew, "Stretch Armstrong" had me wrapped up in a great, big, bear hug. We were two complete strangers brought together by a handful of handwritten words my cousin had penned earlier that day. From the corner of my eye, I saw looks of confusion from Mom, my cousin and my aunt. The three later professed that they had braced for a fight, had it come to that.

I can laugh about it now because, as it turns out, Jeremiah (i.e., Stretch Armstrong) is really just a big-hearted softy whose bark is much worse than his bite. He shared with me how that Love Note saved him. He often says, "Natalie, you will never know how many lives your Love Notes have saved."

Jeremiah is a US Army veteran who fought a long and difficult battle just to get into the military. Having donated one of his kidneys to his mother years prior, he needed a letter from the surgeon general, himself, allowing him to serve his country with one good kidney. Being the kind of guy who doesn't take no for an answer, Jeremiah got that letter from the surgeon general and was soon shipped out to a warzone in Iraq as an MP.

For his trouble, he returned stateside with post-traumatic stress and a traumatic brain injury sustained during an ambush while in-country. He has since medically retired and, for some time, struggled to receive the care needed to recover.

I think that parking lot hug was *the* moment I realized these Love Notes were not just fluff—cutesy hearts and flowers sent into the great, wide void. They were loaded weapons of mass appreciation, aimed straight for the hearts of our heroes, and if they could break down the walls of one angry veteran in a grocery store parking lot in a matter of moments, what could they do for the lot of them over time?

This was not nothing.

Jeremiah, now a local firefighter and family man, became my first *real* follower—if you don't count Mom. He is like family to me, and he is a big proponent of this mission. He speaks with me on its behalf to businesses and schools and to whomever will listen.

Just the other day, almost five years since that parking lot hug, Jeremiah, (JD as his friends affectionately call him), sent me a text message out of the blue. It read: *"Natalie, I just want you to know I appreciate you. Even though you're not here [in Arizona], you still inspire me and still make me truly believe that people do care, and I am not alone. I am coming on shift this morning and am having a really hard time—not doing good. I open my locker at work and the first thing I see is a note from you. So, thank you, Natalie, for being you. I love you so much and thank God every day to have you in my life, and that so many others have you in theirs. I wish I could give you another parking lot hug right now. I really need it."*

The timing of this particular text message was unbelievable. I was having a rotten day, and it was proof positive that the love you put out into the world will always find its way back to you—just in time, too.

We live in a world that is becoming more and more disconnected every day. According to the Centers for Disease Control and Prevention, of the 1.4 million attempts, there were 48,344 people in the United States who committed suicide in 2018—800,000 worldwide.

Again, that's not nothing.

It's worth mentioning that nearly every single Love Note recipient that has ever reached out to me, thus far, affirmed that they needed that small handwritten vote of confidence in that moment, which leads me to believe that we *all* could use a little love on any given day, at any given moment. And, honestly, writing and delivering these Love Notes has been the easiest thing—easier than ordering a cup of coffee these days. On top of which, it has been healing, on so many levels. If we hope to save the world, we need only take the time to show up for those within arm's reach, whether we know them or not. *That* is our collective superpower.

I parked at Target to wait for my wife to pick up some allergy medication. As I waited, a lady approached my driver window with this envelope. She said that she noticed my veteran plates and had these notes ready to give to the veteran drivers. Faith in humanity restored. I'm certainly not one of those vets that feels comfortable receiving thanks, let alone receiving a wonderfully constructed sentiment of genuine appreciation. But politics and personal differences aside, human kindness can bridge our gaps. Thank you, Ms. Natalie, wherever you are. You're a beautiful person and this act of kindness put an angry veteran's cold heart back in its place.

—Mark W., USMC

FIVE

The Secret Sauce

I am the wordiest, nerdiest girl you are likely to meet. Since I could hold a No. 2 pencil in my pudgy, little hand, words have been my thing. I can almost touch and taste them. The way in which flowers intuitively chase sunlight, I chase sentences and stories. I was told that I inherited my love of words from my Grandpa Hirni—my dad's dad.

I kind of dig that!

Since I didn't inherit his artistic talent for oil painting and carving, I am most grateful for his love of the written word. I suppose that's why I went against my high school guidance counselor's advice and remained devoted to a writing career. It has afforded me many handsome breaks, literally and figuratively, none more handsome than my last book deal, but I'll get to him in a bit.

A few months prior to Valentine's Day 2016, I toyed with the idea of writing random notes to strangers, leaving them strewn about town. I was looking for something, (anything!) to keep me focused on the good stuff, complete with famous quotes and positive affirmations. Mom's cancer was all-consuming.

I needed a lifeline.

I had no real plan of erecting an entire mission. I was simply planting a seed, hoping something positive would grow from it. It wasn't until Mom and I began writing to veterans and first responders that I realized that we were on to something special, and that this simple gesture could, indeed, be a force for good. And, so, I slapped a hashtag on it, still not knowing where we were going.

Mom wasn't too keen on the name Nothing but Love Notes in the beginning. It was a little too "mushy and romantic" for her taste, but I liked it, and so it stuck because, 1.) I wanted this act of kindness to be known for love—nothing more, nothing less. 2.) I wanted the gesture to be circulated in the breadth of a handwritten note. And, so, there it was, our purpose staring back at us.

Suddenly, life came into focus, and even though I didn't have an official "plan of attack" for this undertaking, Mom and I took to writing Love Notes every single day. That was the mission at hand. We'd start off most mornings at our local Starbuck's, armed with coffee and card stock. It was just the two of us, and it was so cathartic. Not only were we having conversations with the locals in our community, but we were having a priceless mother-daughter dialogue at a time when it mattered most. I will never forget those precious mornings spent writing with her. It gave us both something hopeful to focus on. Doing something meaningful with our hands made all the difference. We were much happier, not to mention healthier. That's not to say it was always easy to focus on the bright side. It wasn't, but it helped—a lot!

Writing Love Notes to strangers was such a little thing—a long shot in the grand scheme. There were days when I wondered if it was enough, but the truth was, this small act was a surprising cure on so many levels, starting with Mom's prognosis. From there, it led to the healing of a daughter's broken heart, a veteran's troubled mind and beyond. Love Notes invited conversation into our day, a much-needed exchange between humans. In hearing other people's stories, we didn't feel so isolated in our own. It was beginning to feel a bit like fate, a calling that wouldn't let us go.

Here's the thing about fate; it brings with it a big ask. It all but demands that a girl act from a place of courage, stepping forward in faith with that which God has planted in her heart. This isn't always easy, especially when the girl is in a severe holding pattern, circling the drain with little to no resources. Sometimes destiny finds her at her worst, at a time when life has just about got her licked. And then, suddenly from out of nowhere, providence steps in and not a moment too soon.

Thank God for small favors.

I was working at Mary Lou Fulton Teachers College at Arizona State University. I had a good-looking corner office with a magnificent view of Fletcher Lawn. Two of my walls were picture windows that faced the Fletcher Library and a beautiful cobalt-blue, half-moon reflecting pool. On the outside, one might assume that my salary was just as impressive as my view.

As if.

I was making less than half of what I made at American Express, living paycheck to paycheck. I had convinced myself that the cool corner office at the nation's number one university for innovation was enough.

It wasn't.

Thanks to cancer, I had clarity. It had been almost one year since Mom's diagnosis. I was taking a lot of time off from work to care for her, when it occurred to me that it might be time to quit the "day job." The timing was far from perfect, but is there ever an ideal time to chase a dream? It's kind of like choosing to have children. If you wait for the perfect time, it'll never happen. Sometimes you've got to go for broke—bite the bullet, grab the bull by the horns and just go for it. So, I played around with the idea of submitting my resignation. I tinkered with the numbers, and I quickly realized, less the health benefits, I could make the same money working as a substitute teacher. This would allow me the freedom to pick and choose my gigs, giving me more time to care for Mom and, of course, muster this new mission of mine. Although I'd never been without health benefits, I was feeling energized at the thought.

Mom didn't like the idea of me leaving ASU. She loved bragging to her friends that her daughter worked at a university. Forget the fact that my heart wasn't in it. What I lacked was purpose, a feeling of fulfillment at the end of the day. I knew that if I were to leave, I would be surrendering all the advantages of a good job.

That's not what scared me.

What scared me was missing out on the chance to spend my

time and what little resources I had, on that which mattered most, Mom and our mission. Don't get me wrong, it was tempting to settle, to stick to what *seemed* certain at the time, especially since I had no idea how to make this new venture work. And, so, I stopped worrying about the "how," and shifted that unconstructive energy to the bigger question: *"Why?"*

Somewhere deep in my heart I knew that this was *my* path. From there, it was baby steps and a simple matter of faith. Remember, all a girl needs is "faith the size of a mustard seed." Besides that, it was already becoming abundantly clear that the more love I gave, the more I got in return, and that, in and of itself, was *the* greatest resource I had going for me.

Love is the secret sauce.

With Mom's prognosis, there was no time to waste. God had planted this seed in my heart, and I was going to find a way to make it happen—come hell or high water. As tempting as it was, my destiny was not to be squandered binge-watching Netflix or going with the flow.

Talk about terrible time sucks!

I was like salmon. I needed to exert energy, swim against the current, so to avoid being swept downstream. God had bigger plans for me, and it was in those dark days that I happened upon *the* great love story of my life. It would have been much easier to zone out and get sucked into yet another season of Sons of Anarchy while killing myself with carbs and Coca Cola, but instead I put on my big-girl pants and summoned the courage to do something bigger.

That was it—the inspiration. From there, Mom and I turned off the television and started giving love away—freely, without condition and from out of our own pocket. It's not that we cooked up some elaborate scheme to change the world, even though it started to look that way. All we did was deliver love where it was needed, and we were persistent, passionate, inspired and resourceful about it. Nothing half ass here.

We never let up or let on that life had us beat. No matter how bad it hurt or how insignificant the work seemed or what anyone else said to try and detour us, we persisted. The magic was in the giving. The miracle was in the believing, and the healing was in the handwriting. There was no denying the abundance of love that was returning to Mom and me because of a Love Note. It was the stuff of miracles. And, so, I had a big decision to make.

Natalie left me a note in Peoria, AZ today at Albertson's parking lot. The note really made my day. I'm a bi-lat combat wounded Army vet amputee. Was shopping and hurting from walking, but the note made it all better. Thanks, Natalie!

—Bradley L., U.S. Army Veteran

SIX
Under the Influence

One of the most telling indicators for success is being under the influence of a great mentor, someone who believes in you and who teaches you *how* to think, not *what* to think. Having someone get behind you, someone whose vast experience and wisdom reinforces and inspires your journey, whatever that may be, could possibly be one of *the* greatest means for achievement.

Honestly, I would never have thought I needed a mentor. It wasn't until one showed up from out of the blue that it occurred to me that I still had *so* much to learn about life and my place in it. The funny thing is, my mentor, a self-made millionaire who would change my life, came looking for me. I was a single, suburban, football mom struggling to make ends meet when this gentleman, a former NBA player and broadcasting businessman, was looking for a writer to pen his life story. Mind you, I had only ever published one children's book and an opinion's column for a local rag. I was college educated, but I didn't have the breadth of experience, let alone the knowledge of how to chronicle (chapter and verse) such a successful guy. In fact, I got a big fat D in a creative writing class in college, mostly because, at nineteen years old, I thought I already knew all I needed to know about storytelling. So, what does the Universe do? It responds with an amazing opportunity.

This is the "big ask" I was talking about.

Destiny doesn't wait until the timing is right or until you have all your ducks in a neat, little row or you get an A+ in creative writing. Sometimes it comes calling when you are least expecting.

Not long before Mom was diagnosed with cancer, I received a phone call from a former co-worker and a good friend named Caroline. She was working for one of the big hospitals in Scottsdale.

"One of our philanthropists is looking for a writer to author his autobiography," she said. "He's led an incredible life. He played and coached college basketball. He was drafted into the NBA and, ultimately, retired at 43 years old, having made his fortune in radio."

"Oh my," I replied. "That's amazing!"

"Yes, and, of course, I thought of you."

You thought of me?

"Send him your resume," she insisted. "His name is Bob Duffy. He's a great guy. He's very smart and charismatic. You'll love him."

Half-heartedly, I promised Caroline that I would reach out to this man, but the truth is I lacked confidence. That's a terrible deficiency to have, especially when opportunity presents itself. But here's the thing: When opportunity knocks, whether you think you are ready for it or not, **BELIEVE THAT YOU ARE**! Otherwise, these big breaks might pass you by. And the "what ifs" are just too big a price to pay for it. Besides, what's the worst that can happen?

You fall on your face?

The truth is, I had been preparing for this opportunity my whole life, but do you think I called the man?

I did not.

Doubt got the better of me, and I totally chickened out.

I know. I know.

I had more cluck than pluck that day. Something big was happening, but I failed to act. I mean, if I had tried to solicit this opportunity on my own, it never would have happened. I wasn't proud of myself for chickening out. In fact, I tried not to think about it over the next few days.

A lot of good that did.

Thankfully, the Universe gave me another shot. Two weeks later, I received a phone call from the man himself—Bob Duffy. In that brief conversation, Bob shared with me bits and pieces of his remarkable story, spanning the course of many years and a handful of incredible careers. I let him talk me into lunch to discuss the project. It must have been all that charisma Caroline was talking about. The truth is I still wasn't sure I had it in me to write this book, but I owed it to myself (and to him) to take the meeting.

Self-doubt be damned.

I walked into the Scottsdale restaurant like I owned the joint, a lioness on the prowl, boldly traipsing across the Savannah, going in for the kill. I looked as if I knew exactly what I was doing. *I didn't have a clue.*

What I did have was a smart portfolio and a brave face. I glanced around the restaurant and caught the gaze of a handsome, well-dressed gentleman sitting at a large, half-moon booth. My heart was pumping double-time. Bob stood up, as I approached. He had on an expensive sweater that matched his bright blue eyes and accentuated his million-dollar smile.

"Thanks for coming," he said, extending his hand.

"Of course," I replied, sounding awfully convincing, considering my knees were twitching nervously.

The moment he took my hand, there was instant rapport. Bob has a way about him that puts people at ease. Caroline was right. He was charismatic, which may or may not have had something to do with his unbelievable success.

"Can I get you something cool to drink," the waiter asked, handing me a menu. I glanced to see what Bob was drinking—scotch on the rocks. It was official. I was sitting at the grownup table. I considered ordering something smart, like a Cosmo or a vodka martini—neat. However, being the quintessential "cheap date," a girl who cannot hold her liquor, I opted for a drink I knew I could stomach *without* having to be slung over the waiter's shoulder at the end of the meeting.

"I'll have a Coca Cola, please," I smiled, feeling a little green around the edges. "On the rocks!"

Bob smiled and the waiter chuckled.

Just breathe.

In the first ten minutes of that two-hour luncheon, I knew I had to take on this book project. Much like Gandalf in The Hobbit, Bob's great strength is in revealing, as well as reinforcing the innate superpower of mere mortals like me. He was presenting the call to adventure, and I was compelled to answer. I felt his confidence in me almost immediately. I couldn't let him down.

I wouldn't.

That's not to say I wasn't scared to death.

I was.

I was also asking myself the question, *Am I good enough?*

The self-doubt came in waves throughout that meeting, flushing out what little confidence I had. One minute I was sure of myself, the next I was my own worst skeptic. I had to remind myself that I grew up working for businessmen like Bob at American Express. I had been professionally groomed for this opportunity. On top of which, there was my experience as a columnist for the Arizona Republic, to say nothing of my innate gluiness, that stubborn part of me that has got no quit.

I'm the girl who gets her goat!

And, if that wasn't enough, I could always lean on my education. I graduated cum laude in Communication. I was ready for this.

No. I was born for this.

Bob had complete faith in my ability, which went a long way considering his vast experience and success. He helped me see something in myself that I hadn't fully seen before—promise. Over the course of the next three years, Bob and I wrote his book, from his humble childhood to his million-dollar philanthropic endeavors.

We met for lunch once, sometimes twice, a week, alternating between his two beautiful homes in Carefree and Flagstaff, as well as our two favorite restaurants— The White Chocolate Grill and The Capital Grille. It was always good company and  smart conversation, complimented by a feast fit for a king. I think I put on ten pounds writing that book, but overall, knowing Bob changed my life. It changed my outlook, and it certainly changed my trajectory. I can honestly say that "Nothing but Love Notes" would not have happened, if not for this man's love, encouragement, and support. He believed in me when I didn't believe in myself.

Three years later, our book was finished. It was aptly titled, *Make it Happen*. Bob and I sat down over a celebratory dinner at The Capital Grille. We were in the middle of our meal—Lobster Bisque and a mouth-watering, Bone-in Kona Crusted Dry-Aged New York Strip with Shallot Butter—when Bob leaned across the table with a warm smile and said, "Natalie, my wish for you is that our book leads you to bigger things."

Huh?!

"With all due respect, Bob," I said, washing down a thick cut of New York strip with a big gulp of Cabernet Sauvignon. "How could it get any bigger than this?"

"You know," Bob smiled. "The last time I sat in this booth, I was having lunch with Bruce Halle, the billionaire founder of Discount Tire. He was sitting right where you are now, in that very seat. You are something special, Natalie … and I am convinced that there is nothing Bruce did in his life and career that you can't do."

A colossal lump caught in my throat. I couldn't tell if it was a big, hunk of beef that had gotten lodged or my heart was swelling into the size of my fist. So, I quickly excused myself, lest I lose my composure or consciousness, depending on what was currently compromising my airway.

As I pushed past the heavy wooden door leading into the ladies' room, I stepped into the warmest, amber light. The bathrooms in this joint are phenomenal. Tears trickled down my cheeks. I stepped up to the vanity mirror, just as a tall, elegant woman wearing a white, linen dress was finishing her face. After smearing on a coat of Coco Chanel's rouge lip color, she blotted her full, red lips with a fresh tissue. Her hazel eyes were drawn to my reflection, as she capped the expensive cosmetic. She was lovely. I struggled to look away.

The corners of her bright, red lips curled upward, as she

turned to leave. My eyes turned to my own reflection in the mirror. I looked different, not on the outside, but on the inside. I could see it, clear as day. Something exuded from the wet, green eyes looking back at me. It may have just been the blur from the tears, but I saw fearlessness. I had done what I did not think I could do.

After lightly dabbing my wet cheeks with the back of my hand, I applied a fresh coat of Burt's Bees Plum Lip Shimmer—the broke girl's answer to Coco Chanel. The truth was, I didn't feel broke. I felt like a million bucks. My lip balm might not have had the same luminous intensity of the woman in the white dress, but the confident curl in my smile was no less compelling.

Bob believed in me.

That meant more to me than he would ever know. I can't say that I ever got that brand of approval from my own dad, which can do a real number on a girl's self-confidence and self-worth. Bob's unwavering belief in me gave me courage, and his influence made me dangerous. I wouldn't be founding the next big tire company anytime soon, but I was definitely on my way to becoming a big wheel in my own way.

And Bob's book did, indeed, lead to bigger things. It led me to a fruitful freelance writing career that paid handsomely, not just in income, but in love, support and friendship. It led me to two more writing gigs, both of which came looking for me based on Bob's generous recommendation. The first was a professional soccer player whose David and Goliath-like tale taught me a great lesson in courage and persistence.

The second was Carol Latham, a Silicon Valley phenom whose invention changed technology as we know it. When she was my age, in the early 90s, she invented a ceramic material that keeps computer chips cool, like the one you are holding in your hand right now. Yes, your cell phone doesn't overheat because of something this lady (Carol!) created. I admire how she fought to keep her intellectual property and her wits about her in an industry where women were few and far between. Her story got a little dicey there for a minute, but she held her ground and, indeed, turned out a product that cools technology. That's all I want, to put out a product that is meaningful to the world, only I want to warm the hearts of those humans holding the technology. I think God put Carol in my life for a reason. I know He did.

Over the course of a few months, while editing her book, we became fast friends. I just love her! She has given me something I lost a few years ago, a voice of reason and the kind of love that is unquestionable. As a matter of fact, each of these three mentors have been quite inspiring, each in their own way. They came into my life at just the right time, changing me and expanding my options and courage exponentially. Knowing them, ultimately, prepared me for the fourth (and biggest) book deal of my career to date—in more ways than one. And, to think, if I hadn't found the courage to accept

Bob's book deal in the beginning, none of the doors that followed would have been there for me to venture into.

I see what you did, God.

As Bob walked me to my car that night, I told him about my idea for Love Notes. He sensed my trepidation when I mentioned quitting my job at ASU to pursue Mom's palliative care and my mission to show gratitude to our nation's heroes. He also recognized how I lit up and the excited tone in my voice when I shared stories of my encounters.

"I know quitting my job is irresponsible and completely ridiculous," I said. "But I feel something tugging at me to do it."

"Natalie," Bob said, smiling and warmly placing his hand on my shoulder. "There's no such thing as job security. Nothing in this life is guaranteed, not even a good university job. *You* are your best and safest bet. Making the right decision for *your* life means taking calculated risks. If this mission and your mom's palliative care means that much to you, you have an obligation to do whatever it takes to make it happen."

It was exactly what I needed to hear. One grateful hug and a few days later, I submitted my resignation at Arizona State University, and I never looked back.

Thank you, Bob! I love you.

Natalie, it was 10:45 or later Monday morning when I walked out of my psychiatrist office after 45 minutes of an emotionally-draining session. I found myself in the lobby (I don't know why). When you came into the VA Center in Anthem, AZ, you said something nice to me and handed me a card and then left. I didn't take much notice of what you handed me at first, but sitting in my car I opened the little envelope with pretty stars on it and removed one of the largest gifts I have ever received. Your thank-you note was so touching that I sat and cried for 155 minutes before I could even drive. Just noticing it on the table still brings me to tears (of emotional release) almost a week later. I never heard anything like that during the Nam War, quite the contrary! Again, thank you so much! God bless you.

—Don I., Vietnam Veteran

SEVEN

The Last Ten Dollars

T he day I met Elise was one of *the* biggest blessings of my life, for a couple of reasons. Firstly, she is like a soul sister, and secondly, knowing Elise has helped me develop a whole new kind of courage, priming me for a life I didn't even know I would want to be a part of.

Hand on heart, I can honestly say that she is *the* tie that binds me to all that is good in my life today, including two of *the* biggest loves of my life, but I'll get to that a little bit later.

Elise found me through a friend, a firefighter who had received one of my Love Notes. Curious, she looked up our hashtag (#nothingbutlovenotes) and started following our Facebook page. I'll never forget the day she reached out. The timing couldn't have been better or worse, depending on how you looked at it.

She wrote: *Hey! I know you don't know me. My name is Elise, and you left my friend (who is a fireman) a letter on his car. I started following you because it is such a great thing! Thanks for all you do! I wanted to let you know that there is a fundraiser tonight at Barro's Pizza. I serve on the board for the Peoria Police Citizen's Academy Alumni. We fundraise for our non-profit and give to the*

Peoria Police Department. Just wanted to let you know because I know you are a supporter for first responders. I'll message you the flyer, so you'll know the details. If you go, make sure you find me!

As I read the details on the flyer, I looked at the time. It was four o'clock in the afternoon. The fundraiser was set to start in one hour. That day, I had hit a mental and emotional wall. Mom wasn't feeling great either.

We were kind of a mess.

I had just quit my job at ASU the day before. I had ten dollars in my pocket (less than that in my bank account after paying the mortgage). The one bright spot, after having cashed out my modest retirement fund, was that there was a check in the mail for six-grand with my name on it.

While the invitation was a perfect opportunity to connect with my community, I wasn't in the mood for mingling. I was, however, happy that Elise reached out. It was proof, we were making an impact. I read the message to Mom. She was sitting on the sofa opposite me, and even though she wasn't feeling good, it didn't keep her from inserting her two cents.

"You're going to that fundraiser," she said.

"Mom, I have ten dollars to my name and nothing to wear," I whined, sinking deeper into the sofa. "I'm not going."

"You *are* going," she insisted. "If you mope around here, like you only have ten dollars in your pocket, that's how people will perceive you, **BUT** if you walk into that fundraiser looking like a million bucks, then *that's* how they will distinguish you."

"Mom …"

"Go doll yourself up. Brush your hair. Put on a cute outfit and lipstick. Show up to this thing looking like you own the place."

In other words, straighten your crown, daughter!

Mom smiled her knowing smile. As usual, she knew exactly what I needed—fresh air, new faces, a swift kick in the pants, a slice of pizza … and, of course, lipstick.

The truth was my house was beginning to feel sick. The air was stale. Mom's clothes and skin smelled sour from the chemo. Some days it was hard to breathe. Cancer treatment is a miserable adventure. I don't recommend it.

As I made my way to my bedroom to change, Mom pushed herself up off the couch and slowly ambled to her room and said, "I'm going with you, if it's the last ten dollars we spend."

I tried feigning confidence, as I walked into the local pizza joint. I ordered two slices of pepperoni pizza with a couple of Cokes to wash it down. I handed the cashier my last ten-

dollar bill and, so as not to appear as though it was a big deal, I told her to keep the change. It wasn't much, but it was for a couple of good causes. Firstly, and most importantly, it was in support of our local police department, and secondly, it got Mom and me out of the house and into a better frame of mind.

We needed it!

Mom and I slipped into a booth with our meal, and I quietly prayed it wasn't our last.

O ye, of little faith!

We chatted away, as if nothing in our lives was uncertain, as if I hadn't handed out my last Hamilton and Mom wasn't dying. I was suddenly grateful that Mom forced the issue of getting us out of the house and into our community. That was the *one* thing that

continued to rescue me throughout our whole ordeal—giving back.

It wasn't long before Elise approached our table and introduced herself. She and I hit it off right away. We discussed our shared love of first responders. I shared with her mine and Mom's love story. Elise and I have been as thick as thieves since that August day in 2016, and I can honestly say, those (last) ten dollars was the best money I ever spent because 1.) I was immediately reminded of my self-worth, and 2.) It led me to a life (and a love) that I am totally crazy about. All things considered ... ten bucks was a total bargain.

Natalie, people like you make our community and our world a better place. Thank you! For being a voice of Love, Gratitude, *and Positivity! I can't wait to meet you in person. Until then, I hope this little gesture helps keep your mission going.*

—Mylinda F., LEO Wife & Mom

EIGHT
Two Birds

I knew that Elise and I would be famous friends when we were at an active-shooter training for our local police department. As the scenario began, and we were waiting for SWAT to storm in to our (pretend) rescue, she looked at me from across the room and, in between desperate cries for help, she smiled and said, "This is our real life!"

It was as if she were reading my mind. As she leaned up against the wall with mock gunshot wounds to both legs, and I lay on my back with a feigned sucking chest wound, I knew I had found my place in the world, if not my partner in (mock) crime.

It was such a fun way to give back to the greater good, to those who work so hard to do and be better for the community they protect and serve. I never set out to be a live-action role player (i.e., the designated shooting victim, hostage or bad guy) in SWAT training scenarios, covered in moulage. I didn't even know it was a thing. Elise roped me into it. I simply did my best to show up when they needed me. It was then that the first responders' world opened up to me. Like the pumpkin magically transformed into a carriage for Cinderella, the Love Note miraculously blossomed into an open invitation, a call to action for me to take part in something bigger.

It was a godsend.

It was also really cool. I would often find myself scrunched up in small, cubby holes of vacant buildings, pointing a simulated firearm at a door frame twenty feet away. Because it was so far removed from my everyday life, and so far outside of my comfort zone, it was kind of cathartic. It helped me to be brave. I figured, if I could survive caring for my dying mother and the next ten minutes of this SWAT training scenario, I could survive just about anything.

Nervously, I would wait for our local SWAT team to lumber through the shoot house, like a heat-seeking missile—rifles drawn. I could hear them at the front door. There would be three hard knocks, followed by the booming call out, "Police department! Search warrant! Come out with your hands up!"

As they repeatedly banged on the door and shouted commands, I could feel sweat beading on my forehead, which wasn't surprising since I was encased from head to toe in heavy, protective gear. Every second seemed like an hour, knowing that my assignment was to get a bead on the good guys and engage them.

How did I get here?

Oh, yes! Elise ... the wonderful woman I met because of a firefighter's Love Note. She was the reason I was hunkered down in that musty room with skinny mice darting across the rafters.

*This **was** my real life, but the struggle wasn't real!*

These SWAT trainings turned out to be one of the coolest things I've ever done to support the local first responder community. Seriously! Next to writing Love Notes for these heroes, it is one of my favorite things of all time. It's Elise's favorite, too.

I think she and I were separated at birth.

Elise is that quirky friend who, if you call her up and ask what she is doing, she's likely to tell you, "I'm holding twenty-four people hostage!"

Alongside the Peoria Police Citizens Academy Alumni, this woman has gone to great lengths to provide support to our local law enforcement, including fundraising for bomb dogs, roleplaying for SWAT trainings and providing holiday meals to on-duty police officers. It's all about the love of local law enforcement, ensuring these good men and women have what they need to do their job.

It's her thing ... her love note.

Hairstylist by day, live-action role player by night—Elise found a fun way to give back to her community, and she includes me and a handful of her other friends, making it even more fun. And, as if it couldn't get any better than that, we were told SWAT trainings are much more effective when there are real, flesh-and-bone bodies in play vs. paper targets and dummy victims.

I love our nation's first responders with all my heart, and I would do anything to see that they get the training they need, especially if it gets them home safe at the end of their shift. That matters to me in a big way, and I am willing to do my part to make it happen. People often ask how much role players are compensated for their time and trouble, to which I reply, "Well, sometimes we get to barbecue hot dogs and hamburgers with the SWAT team."

Oh, the baffled looks I get.

I think what people fail to realize is that the more you give, the more you get. It's not about the payday. It's about paying it forward. Honestly, these days I am more interested in action than reaction. The difference between the two is vast—everything online is reaction. Showing up in person is action. Between the two, only one actually ever accomplishes anything.

Much like Mom, I know that one day I will leave this earth, and I don't plan on leaving anything on the field, except for a footprint of love, hope and gratitude. That, for me, is what I gained from having lost one of the great loves of my life. That, and the fact, that we are all in this together. Much like writing Love Notes, my days spent training with Elise and our local law enforcement has shown me what it truly takes to make a difference.

Funny story: At one of the last active-shooter trainings I attended with Elise, the instructor was speaking to a large group of SWAT operators from around the state. He mentioned that there were two bothersome birds, pigeons I presume, hanging around the training area. The birds were being loud, disruptive and pooping on everything. He shared how the training staff had tried scaring them off with Simunition rounds and rocks, anything to get them to fly away. However, no matter what they did, the two birds stayed put. As the large group of men laughed out loud, I glanced over at Elise and whispered, "Is he talking about us?"

We still laugh about that to this day, but the truth is, like those two birds, it's going to take a whole lot more than a few (stinging) Simunition rounds and rocks to get rid of the two of us.

These trainings mean the world to Elise and me, as do the men and women who are training. And I know for a fact that our being there means something to them, too, especially if it gets them back into the waiting arms of those they love at the end of their shift.

Kaw. Kaw. That's bird-speak for "I love you, Elise!"

Dear Natalie, I would like to thank you and Nothing but Love Notes for your words of sympathy in our time of sadness. Your kindness brings us great comfort as we grieve Officer Conrad Gary and Officer Eduardo Marmolejo. With gratitude.

—Eddie T. Johnson, Superintendent, Chicago Police Dept.

NINE

My Superpower

Thereisa Turkish proverb that reads: "*Kind words will unlock an iron door.*" If there's one lesson from my Love Note experience that I like to pass onto others, above all else, it is that. I believe most of the ills in the world would be best served through kindness and compassion. It sounds a little simplistic and naïve.

I know.

But I have seen big, strong, (sometimes angry) men, wounded war veterans and police officers who have survived the worst of the worst in war and violence, weep after reading a few simple, handwritten words of love and gratitude. I have looked into their softening, wet eyes, wrapped my arms around their thick, quivering shoulders, and did my very best to hold them together. I make grown men cry. Therefore, I am.

Me. The girl who needs help opening a pickle jar.

I deliver just a little bit of hope and love in the breadth of a handwritten Love Note while in line at the grocery store, at a local coffee shop, in an airport terminal, at a friend's backyard barbeque or at a fallen officer's funeral. I keep these notes in my purse, wherever I go. When I cross paths with a military serviceman, a veteran or a first responder, I let them know that they are loved and that they are not alone—better now than never.

This brand of love does not serve our heroes well if we save it for after they've fallen. If we wait for the funeral, it will have been too late. That outpouring of love and reverence at a hero's burial, while poignant and beautiful, is for those of us left behind, not the ones we've lost. The brand of love I deliver is in the moment—the here and now. It  is honest and true, and, except for the price of a greeting card, it comes at no cost. And per Mom's request, we are to expect nothing in return.

It's not lost on me, however, that most Love Note recipients are only too happy to return the favor with love, hugs and thanks of their own. Oftentimes, they offer friendship, which, in and of itself, is a gift. To tell you the truth, the act of writing Love Notes and the heartfelt blowback that occurs because of it, feels so darn good. Most days I feel selfish.

No, really!

These Love Notes have struck a chord in the hearts of our heroes and the communities they serve, exposing them for what we all are—human! The fact that a Love Note got my mom out of bed and out of her sick and worried mind during the last two years of her life, said it all. She was *the* strongest woman I knew, a rock, but life (and a terminal cancer diagnosis) got the better of her. She hit a wall and fell into a depression. It was because of a Love Note, and her daughter's innate gluiness, that her purpose was reborn. It rehabilitated her outlook, and I can honestly say that it gave us both reason to get out of bed in the morning.

For the most part, we all want the same things from life, not the least of which is love and understanding. We all want to be seen, heard and felt during our short stay here on Earth. I have found that if you are real with people, and if you take the time to show up, demonstrating how much better the world (your world!) is because of them, you will not only make a profound impact on their day, but you will have made a profound impact on your life. Like forgiveness, gratitude is a gift you give yourself.

It is the stuff of miracles.

I'm not just shoveling sunshine here. These Love Notes saved my life, and I believe they have the power to restore humanity. I look around, and I see a world divided, and rather than search for ways to connect with one another at a deeper, more human level, we (as a society) rush to judgement. We are inclined to go straight for the jugular with bared teeth, as if any one of us is better than the other. We'll never find peace and happiness that way. Kicking someone, while they are up or down, is ***not*** a sign of a happy person.

These Love Notes, as arbitrary as they are, have an honesty about them, a kindness that catches people off guard. They create much-needed conversation and, ultimately, reveal our vulnerability. It's ironic, really. It took our nation's best and bravest to show me what it means to be vulnerable. By bearing their souls and their scars, both seen and unseen, they allowed me to do the same.

Like my mother, I am strong to a fault. I have always saved my tears and fears for when I am alone, usually locked behind the bathroom door in a hot tub of bubbles at the end of the day. Nowadays, I can be found weeping in the arms of our heroes in the middle of coffee shops, restaurants, and on airplanes 30,000 feet in the air.

Not one of us is above suffering, not even our strongest men and women in uniform. Like the rest of us, they hurt. Some of them deeply, in places we don't even know about. Because they appear so strong and resilient on the surface, we hesitate to say thank you or to ask how they are doing. Because, like every law enforcement officer I've ever met, we assume they are "good to go."

Don't let the badge, the Kevlar and the sidearm fool you.

Our uniformed heroes have gotten good at holding it together. These humans whose job it is to protect and serve need love and gratitude more than we know. There is a reason they put on a brave face. It is for the sake of staying strong, so that they can effectively stay in the fight, respond to the next call, go into battle. It makes sense, but over time, that warrior mentality can, and will catch up to them.

At a time when we are most connected, digitally speaking, real human connection, the kind that we all long for, if not live for, is wasted because there is no text message, email or chatbot that can compete with the amount of ink it takes to simply say "Thank you" and "I love you." That, and the face-to-face interaction that follows, is what moves and inspires people. Handwriting is a dying art, and if lost, I fear could be detrimental to the human spirit.

As many of these interactions as I've had, and there have been many, I will never forget the names and faces of those men and women who opened their hearts to me. When I cross paths with our first responders and veterans, especially the older (forgotten) generations, I can almost picture them in their youth—handsome, uniformed servicemen standing before me, wearing their hearts on their sleeve. They walk among us, but they won't be here forever. And as they proudly recount their service from decades gone by, their milky eyes twinkle, and their sunken chests puff out. I don't take any of these connections for granted—not one. I remember them all. *That* is my superpower.

My parents got one of these on their car today. I am their son, their Marine, and I can't express how grateful I am to see that note. I am not home with them, as I am stationed somewhere else. But still very heartwarming and in my four years, and about to go on my second deployment, it's the first time I have received thanks for my service, and I don't truly know how to respond other than thank you. I will surely have this note my whole life.

—Corporal Caparell, USMC

TEN
Breaking the Ice

I spent a lot of time alone, writing Love Notes at Starbuck's. For some time, it was my form of therapy—a refuge, really. Like clockwork, I'd show up at my usual haunt, commandeering my usual corner booth. I'd order my usual poison—trenta strawberry refresher, hold the berries. I'd sit down and take to handwriting Love Notes to America's heroes. I played with different types of ink pens and card stock, stickers and stationery. I made sure that each note felt personal, as if handwritten specifically with one person in mind. Throughout Mom's illness and even after losing her, this gesture kept me focused on the good stuff, on the good people in my community and on the good fight. The effort, itself, felt worthwhile. That's not to say there weren't days I questioned my sanity.

I did ... and often.

Everything in my life was up in the air—my career, my direction, my finances, my sense of purpose. I didn't know it at the time but starting this mission would lead me down an unexpected road to recovery. It was *the* quintessential "road less traveled," which is probably why most of the time I was shlepping it alone. I would often send out invites on Facebook and Instagram, inviting people to join me. I had no idea if anyone was even listening, but I figured I would put the word out and hope for the best. Most of the time it was just me.

Party of one.

I suppose, if a girl is serious enough about making an impact, she is willing to stand alone and, perhaps, even look ridiculous. Looking ridiculous was never a problem for me. I never really cared what people thought. Mom used to say I was shameless, to which I would always reply, "You say that like it's a bad thing."

Every now and again someone would show up to write with me, which was always comforting. Whether it was a friend, a family member, or a complete stranger, there was a community developing. It took some time, but eventually people started reaching out, requesting Love Note writing sessions for specific heroes—fallen and/or sick. I loved that people trusted me in that way.

I don't take that for granted.

Since spear-heading this mission, I have yet to experience a true adverse response. I did have one police officer flat out refuse a Love Note, but I didn't take it to heart. I got the feeling he was having a rotten day, which, ironically, made him a perfect mark, but you can't win them all. I also had one woman sitting at a table next to me reject the opportunity to write a Love Note for a law enforcement officer for fear it would get into the "wrong hands."

Come again.

After I explained to her what it is we do and why, I posed the question again, "Would you like to contribute a handwritten

Love Note for our law enforcement community? They could use it right now."

To my surprise, she still refused. That almost never happens. The woman scoffed, "Not unless you can guarantee me it will get into the hands of a police officer who *actually* deserves it. I mean, they can't all be good cops."

Wait. What?!

"Well, isn't *that* what love is?" I probed. "Giving someone what they need most, even if they deserve it least?"

I believe it's called the benefit of the doubt.

The woman vehemently shook her head, and through pursued lips replied, "I'll pass!"

She looked perturbed, as if I had asked her to donate a kidney to her worst enemy. It was all I could do to smile and thank her for her time.

Geesh, lady!

The trouble is, some let the high court of public opinion get in the way of a good deed, forgetting that we are all just one kind gesture away, as random as it may be, from turning a negative condition on its ear. I've seen it happen. Kindness cuts right to the chase. Choosing to refrain from random kindnesses, based on one's own personal opinion and pain, perpetuates the problem. It's not up to us to decide who deserves love and understanding and who does not. I've seen people's pain up close and personal with this project.

I delivered one Love Note, along with a peanut butter and jelly sandwich, to an angry veteran pan-handling on an extremely busy street corner. His name was Jack. He was an especially large man, 6'6 and no less than 250 pounds. Jack had a giant chip on his shoulder, which made him appear even more considerable in size. I had no business delivering this particular Love Note all by myself, but there was something about him that called to me. Mom was none too happy about it, but I am "gluey" … remember?!

Nevertheless, in just one interaction, this big, angry man melted. We crossed the street, sat down on a curb together and talked in the parking lot of a local home improvement store. While that Love Note didn't solve all of Jack's problems, and there were many, it leveled the playing field between two humans who had absolutely nothing in common, except for the fact that we were both hungry and hurting. We must have been a sight to see.

I visited Jack from time to time. I brought him lunch and, with some help from my followers, bought him a new pair of boots to replace his old, broken-down pair. He returned the favor in a show of respect and gentleness toward me. I won't ever forget that simple exchange and how a Love Note soothed what, on the surface, seemed to be a savaged soul.

In February 2017, I received a message from out of the blue from a dude named Dave. He wrote, "*Just this afternoon, I was made aware of your mission. My brother-in-law received a beautifully-written note from you. I looked at your Facebook page*

and saw a picture of you with a friend of mine, a motorcycle officer. It dawned on me, I should let you know of a large gathering of 911 first responders and vets that happens every Monday morning at Arizona Ice. They play league hockey. I was thinking it could help your mission. Thank you for all that you do to make this country better!"

When I replied with gratitude, Dave responded right away. He appeared extremely grateful and happy to do his part in giving back to the community. After months of pushing the envelope, I was tickled pink to find that people who had not even received a Love Note, but rather were witness to it, were just as moved (if not more inspired) by our mission than those who had. I assured him that I would make a point to stop by the hockey rink to deliver Love Notes to those first responders and veterans.

The very next day I received another message from Dave. He wrote: *"Give me a day to line some stuff up and see what I can come up with, even if it's just a meet and greet. I will be in touch!"*

From there a plot had been hatched—unbeknownst to me. I started receiving daily messages from Dave. I had no idea who this man was or where he came from, but I assumed he must have been Heaven sent, as were most of the people showing up in my life.

Another message from Dave landed in my inbox. It read: *"I spoke with our hockey director, and he is super excited. He will get a hold of the owner and see if he is okay with it, but he thinks he'll love it and will want to be involved. He mentioned February 6th being a great day to do it. So, I'll follow up with him on Wednesday via email and see where we are at."*

The next thing I knew, Dave, a man whose face I wouldn't recognize in a lineup, had arranged an entire event that included an agenda, refreshments, forty first responder and military veteran hockey players, a photographer, a media invite, a local police chief, a local fire chief and the City of Peoria's Vice Mayor Jon Edwards. Except for pulling into the parking lot of the ice rink and seeing the vice mayor slipping into an expensive wool coat, I had no idea this would be anything more than a Love Note delivery on ice.

Instead, Love Notes had broken the ice.

When I showed up to this thing, I only knew about the refreshments and hockey players. I had no idea that there was going to be an entire ceremony in which the City of Peoria's Vice Mayor Jon Edwards would present me with Peoria's Special Citizen Recognition and a Letter of Commendation from Arizona Governor Doug Ducey. I was glad that I had invited my friend Heather to come along for the ride. She is big into hockey, and I thought it would be fun to have her there. I asked Mom and my youngest son to tag along, but they both opted to stay home. Mom later admitted to feeling terrible and crying like a baby that night for not going with me, but how could we have known that Dave had this amazing recognition event up his sleeve?

Again, it just goes to show, if a girl is serious about making an impact, she must be willing to stand alone and, perhaps, even look ridiculous. If you ask me, that's the fun part. Dave and his family have taken me in, as well as taken me ice skating a time or two. His beautiful wife, Erika, has generously created original works of art in support of this mission—window stickers with my hashtag, shadow boxes for wounded police officers, and even t-shirts.

Love begets love, every time!

Thank you for the note. You are truly why we exist.
#devildogs #jarheads

—Anonymous

ELEVEN
Morning Joe

I think it's safe to say that I have hugged more people in the last five years than I have my entire life. When I think of all the crazy connections and conversations that I've had because of a Love Note, I have to pinch myself. We, as humans, are connected by our stories. If we'd only talk to one another, pry open our hearts just a little bit, we might find that we aren't so different.

We are perpetually within arm's reach of good people whose stories resonate with our own. I wish I had a nickel for every time I found myself clutched in the embrace of a stranger in the middle of a crowded coffee shop, in the doorknob aisle at the Home Depot or in the grocery store.

I'd be a wealthy woman.

One Saturday morning I was sitting alone at Starbucks, writing Love Notes, when a young veteran walked in and sat at the table across from me. I spotted him almost immediately. His US Army veteran ballcap gave him away. Unfortunately, I didn't have any veteran Love Notes on me, so I quickly penned one, and as I stuffed it into an envelope with a lick and a prayer, I stood up and walked it over to him. The young man was studying, so I gently slid the note across the table and mouthed the words, "Thank you."

He smiled.

I smiled.

Mission accomplished.

I returned to my table and got back to the business of writing. The coffee shop was slammed that day— standing room only. About an hour later, the young veteran stuffed his books, laptop and unopened Love Note into a rucksack and pushed through the door into a warm, sunny day. Thinking nothing of it, I continued writing and nursing my cool lime refresher (before they discontinued the darn thing).

Ten minutes later, the Army veteran pushed through the front door and made his way back through the crowd. As he drew nearer, I couldn't help but notice that his cheeks were beet red. When he reached my table, he exhaled slowly. He was choked up, so it took him a minute to spit the words out.

"Ma'am," he said, clearing his throat. "Thank you for the note. I read it in my car. It took me a minute to pull myself together, but I wanted to tell you my story, if that's okay."

The blood drained from my face. Suddenly it occurred to

me that these Love Notes might be doing more harm than good to these stalwart soldiers returning home from war. I found my feet and looked him in the eye. He reached out his hand, introducing himself.

"My name is Joe," he said. "I served in the United States Army for eight years. I did two tours in Afghanistan."

Joe halted briefly, taking a combat breath. I squeezed his hand, unable to let it go.

"I lost my best friend, Robert, in an ambush on my last tour," he continued, tears rolling down his cheeks. "He burned to death ... right before my eyes."

The lobby of the coffee shop was buzzing with business. There were people all around us. At its heart, in the center of it all, I wrapped my arms around the young veteran, and we wept together. The rest of the room disappeared.

Joe's shoulders trembled, the same shoulders that carried the immense weight of a military weapon system while in-country, along with the safekeeping of his brothers in arms.

"I'm so sorry," I whispered. "I certainly never meant to stir up all that pain."

Joe shook his head. Feigning a smile and pressing a hard fist to his chest, he said, "Ma'am, you did me a favor. All that pain gets jammed up right here. Your note helped loosen it up a bit."

The mama bear in me squeezed him tight. If only this was a wound mamas like me could kiss and make better. Joe and I spent the next few minutes chatting. It was the next best thing, I imagine.

He told me how he was the one to write home to Robert's

mother, sharing with her how her son lived and how he died courageously for his country. Joe then thanked me in the breadth of another big, bear hug and before I knew it, he was gone.

I haven't seen Joe since that day, but I will never forget his face or his story. He and the many heartfelt hugs that have found me on this journey are never far from my heart. I remember each one of their names and stories.

As if I could forget.

It is because of these infinitely-human interactions that I no longer fear death. The only thing that scares me is not living my life with purpose. I think back to those wasted days when Mom and I binge watched all, but the last season of Sons of Anarchy. She would shake her head and say, "This is so sad. We should be doing more with our lives!"

And do you want to know something? She was right.

As usual.

We could have been doing so much more with our lives, but

better late than never.

Right?

Love Notes became the Litmus Test for my life, in that even without the nickel for every one of these profoundly powerful interactions, I am, indeed, a rich woman!

Dear Natalie, thank you for your support. We love what you do for our community. You have a special place in my heart. I feel that we are somehow connected by dealing with the same situation of family passing from cancer. Thank you so much!

—Reder #76, Westview High School Football

TWELVE

Remission Accomplished

I n discovering our purpose, Mom and I rediscovered each other, only on a whole-new level. Life was looking a little sketchy for us at the start, each of us turning inward as we individually dealt with her cancer diagnosis, but thanks to a Love Note, that all changed.

Our saving grace came to us in the shape of an envelope, and Mom and I pushed it as best we could for as long as we could—together. We spent hours writing at coffee shops and driving around in my Jeep, trolling parking lots, searching for military veterans, police officers and firefighters. It was a scavenger hunt for America's heroes, and in the short season we spent on the road, we fostered an important mother-daughter dialogue that would have been lost, had we stayed holed up at home, one room apart, fearful of the future.

Some days we didn't say much, but it didn't matter because we were in the thick of it together, doing something purposeful with our hands in the face of our greatest adversity. We were unruffled, out in the world, fueled by faith and the occasional conversation with good people in our neighborhood. We were delivering love to a community that needed and deserved it, a community that is too strong to ask for it. And, in effect, *we* were saved. That's not to say that it was easy or that we lost sight of Mom's illness or that life wasn't still throwing hard punches.

It was.

We were simply too focused on our faith (and the task at hand) to let fear get in the way, and in doing so, we created a beautiful chain of events that would change both our lives forever. Mom and I were always tight, but in founding this mission together, we were welded in a way that not even death could destruct.

Mom talked about it for as long as I can remember—a trip to Washington DC. It was on her bucket list. She always loved politics. There were days when she was living with me that she would bat back and forth between CNN and Fox. It was so annoying. Like the NFL, she knew all the players and their stories. I would walk into the room, and she would share with me, blow by (ever-loving!) blow, that which was going down in the White House. Who needed Wolf Blitzer and The Situation Room? I had my mother in my living room, my own personal political correspondent.

I'll never forget the day she called me (crying) because CNN had just aired live-video footage of the USS Philippine Sea steaming toward the Persian Gulf with my firstborn son onboard, delivering the first airstrikes in Iraq. If there was anything going on in the world, Hope knew about it. The woman could speak intelligently on just about any subject.

All that said, I knew this trip to DC had to happen, sooner rather than later. So, I wasted no time in booking reservations. Personally, I didn't have any expectations other than getting her there. I was not about to let this woman leave this earth without visiting our nation's capital. It was her dream.

As we Lyfted into the District of Columbia, I felt a small twinge of excitement when we drove past the Washington Monument, the Lincoln Memorial and the Pentagon. However, the real thrill for me was witnessing Mom's face in the midst of it all. She was all smiles. It was as if she had been transformed, completely removed from the past year—the diagnosis, the treatment, the fear, the pain. At the time, she had achieved temporary remission and had been liberated from treatment for several months. It was a blessing, albeit short-lived. Multiple myeloma is like a bad penny. It keeps turning up.

Anyway, Mom and I spent the next few days tooling around the city on foot. She was still pretty weak, so we went easy. We'd walk around for a while, then stop and rest at a coffee shop or on a park  bench. We'd talk and people watch and sometimes we'd even chat with passersby. Then we'd pick up and go some more.

One day, at a coffee shop near the White House, there were a few Secret Service officers taking a break over coffee and muffins. Mom insisted I give each man a Love Note. Now, these guys were huge, all tact-out in black. I didn't think I had the guts to do it, but how could I not? I had come all that way, and I had not yet given a Love Note to Secret Service. I had to do it! And would you believe? It turned out to be one of my favorite deliveries. One of the officers, whose name was Phil, was even kind enough to take a photo with me. I apologized for being such a groupie, but he assured me that they had been approached by far worse in their line of work, people claiming to have had chips involuntarily implanted inside their head by the government. Suddenly, I didn't feel so silly.

Later that same day, Mom and I sat down in a park just outside of the Lincoln Memorial. We split a tuna-fish sandwich and a bag of potato chips. We washed it down with a couple of ice-cold Cokes. It was a beautiful, autumn day. The sun was shining. Leaves were changing color. People were smiling. Except for a nasty blister on her heel from walking, Mom was feeling pretty good. It all seemed meant to be, especially when a kid on a skateboard zipped by and crash landed on the sidewalk in front of us.

As he checked for scrapes, a woman nearby stood up and offered him a Band-aid—to which he politely refused. As the kid got back on his board and skated off, I intercepted the woman's kind offer with the comment, "My mom could use one."

The woman was only too happy to oblige. Like the paperclip, that bandage showed up just in time. Mom's heel was really blistered and burning, and we had a pretty good walk ahead of us.

As Mom tended to her heel, and I swallowed the last of my sandwich, two big tour buses pulled up and no less than one-hundred veterans disembarked. They slowly headed on foot toward the Vietnam Wall. I looked at Mom, my eyes wide and my backpack bursting at the seams with Love Notes.

"Go get 'em," she said, smiling. "I'll wait here."

I grabbed my backpack and took off like a shot, tracking down as many of the veterans as I could. Most of them were from that era—Vietnam, Korea, World War II. One of the veterans asked if I was a part of the tour, a planned mail call—of sorts.

"Nope," I smiled. "Just some random American girl who is grateful for your service."

The elderly man, who was in a wheelchair, took my hand in his. He squeezed it tight and with tears in his eyes, he whispered, "I would do it all over again for you."

My heart melted. You won't find that feeling of patriotism in history books and certainly not in the news. That's something you've got to go out and get for yourself. In the brief conversations I've had with our military veterans, I've learned more than I ever could have in schoolbooks about America and those who bled for her. The sad truth is these men and women who fought in the World Wars, Korea and Vietnam are vanishing. With each passing day, we are closer to losing these important conversations with them. Their sacrifice is what kept us safe, and their war stories are what bind us to our history and to that which most of us take for granted—freedom. The same is true of all our war veterans.

They are our nation's treasures.

When we returned to the hotel that afternoon, Mom crawled into bed and watched the news for the remainder of the day while nursing a Coke and a big bag of Lay's potato chips—two of her favorites. As for me, I freshened up, downed a big handful of sea-salted almonds and headed back out for a stroll around town. Mom was worried because, in her mind, DC was known for being the "murder capital of the world." If you knew my mom, you would know that was true of any city her daughter was walking through alone. She could be a bit overprotective.

Nevertheless, I spent three good (soulful) hours exploring. I ventured into St. Patrick's Catholic Church on 10th Street. I stood in front of the White House. I bought a big, beef sandwich for a hungry, homeless man. I left Love Notes in my wake—in bicycle baskets, on police cars, on park benches and in the hands of the heroes themselves. My feet and heart ached, but the overall experience was healing.

As I ambled around, I remember feeling a bit lost. None of the streets looked familiar. Each sidewalk presented a new adventure, sometimes beautiful and sometimes precarious. Those long walks in downtown DC changed my perspective on things. I started navigating differently, accepting life's adventure more openly. All too often, we walk around like we have the rest of our lives to venture out of our comfort zone, and the truth is we don't.

All we have is today.

After just a few days, DC had grown on me. It totally took me by surprise. I fell in love with the city. Its patriotism and professionalism are unprecedented. Men wear suits. Women wear pencil skirts with Manolo Blahnik Shushan suede slouchy boots. And just about every man, woman and child respects and salutes the flag. For a girl straight out of suburbia, I found it be one of the sexiest cities in the United States. And, for the record, it was not quite the "murder capital" Mom made it out to be, but that's just me.

Later that night, from the fourth floor, I sat next to the hotel window and people watched. I sat for over an hour, spying on the city's every move. It was cheap entertainment. Every two or three minutes, a story presented itself—a man changing into party clothes from the trunk of his car, a young woman jumping out of a slow-moving vehicle as her boyfriend called out after her, a large, transgender woman strutting across the street wearing nothing more than a thong and high heels, a gaggle of giggling hipsters heading to a local pub.

After watching a young couple kiss, I figured, like a good book, that was a good place to leave off for the night. So, I put on my PJs, brushed my teeth and crawled into bed. It was late, and I was beat. It had been a full few days that included a tour of Arlington Cemetery and a two-hour train ride to Philadelphia (and back) so that I could run the Rocky stairs.

"Good night," Mom whispered.

"Good night," I sighed, turning off the bedside lamp. "I know you think DC is dangerous, but I have never felt safer."

No sooner did I get the words out of my mouth did we hear a blood-curdling scream coming from a woman outside of the hotel. In the inky darkness, Mom and I burst out into gut-wrenching laughter. I nearly wet myself. I was laughing so hard. The two of us giggled all night long. The thought *still* makes me laugh out loud, even as I write this.

These are the moments we would have lost had we not dug deep and found our faith in those dark days. In that way, Mom is still very much present in my life, and it's those stories that keep me connected to her and to my faith that we are all here on purpose, perhaps meant to make life a little bit better for those who are suffering. I know Mom was scared. I could see it in her eyes every so often, in those quiet moments when she was alone in her room, but there was more love than there was fear in those last two years of her life. And there was certainly more laughter.

Natalie, I received your card today. I am a Captain at Buckeye Valley Fire District. After a long day of training recruits on extrication, your simple note of support made my day (month) and gave me that feeling of support and reminded me of why I love my job after fifteen years. I really appreciate all you do, and you truly make a difference. I thank you from the bottom of my heart. You are an angel.

—Dean M., Fire Captain

THIRTEEN

Deathbed Confession

T he cancer had returned. And in the moments that followed Mom's decision to forego further treatment, there was an audible hush at the hospital, along with an instant feeling of relief. Personally, I remember a long exhale. Even though there was a hard goodbye in the pipeline, we could finally put down our swords and rest. The battle was over, in a war that not one of us is going to win, not as mortals. God was calling Hope home, and the only thing left to do was relish our time together—the gap between here and the hereafter.

There wasn't anything more to say or do that we hadn't already said and done. Mom was good about getting stuff off her chest, especially when it came to her children. She didn't believe in holding anything back. She always said exactly what she felt needed to be said, even at the expense of her children's sensibilities. I knew her thoughts on just about every subject, not the least of which was personal safety and beauty. My two personal favorites were: 1.) "Always be aware of your surroundings," and 2.) "Hair scrunchies are for women with no imagination." So, in that regard, those last eleven days were restful and quiet. I was glad for that, and I think Mom was, too.

The last night she spent at the hospital, just before being transferred to Hospice, we were quietly sitting together in her room. I was perched at the foot of her hospital bed, painting her toenails in the spirit of Halloween. The nurses, those earthly angels who are the heart and soul of our health care system, would peek their heads in from time to time to ensure Mom was comfortable. However, they had stopped treating her. That took some getting used to.

Earlier in the day, we heard that Mom's oncologist, Dr. Duck Lips, was making hospital rounds. One of the nurses poked her head in and said, "I'm sure he'll stop in to say hello, Hope."

In hearing this, Mom perked up. She wanted to see him. She waited all day, but he never showed. I was hoping, for no other reason, he would at least give her the dignity of a warm send off.

Yeah. That never happened.

After two years of treating her and making light of her discomfort, Dr. Duck Lip's final snub didn't set well with me. He didn't even have the decency to deliver the news that Mom's cancer had returned and spread to her liver, something I was told never happens with multiple myeloma. Instead, he sent another doctor, a man we'd never met before, to pull me aside and dispense the prognosis. That was a hard conversation to have in a cold hospital corridor. I don't remember hearing anything that man said, except that without treatment Mom would die. And because I knew she was not willing to go through chemo again, I focused my energy on not fainting in front of this good doctor whose bedside manner was much kinder and gentler than Mom's oncologist. I was so grateful for that small show of dignity to Mom and me.

Since that day, I've been meaning to write Dr. Duck Lips M.D. (Mean Doctor) a strongly-worded "Love Note," but I haven't had the heart. I'd much rather save the stamp for something a little more constructive, like a tax payment to the IRS. Being the "Love Note Lady" is perpetual practice in poise. On those days when people irk me, like when they park too close, and I need a can opener to get into my car, it's a good lesson in grace and forgiveness.

Trust me; even Love Note Ladies can lose their cool.

Anyway, in an effort to keep our chins up, I thought it would be fun for Mom and me to have a girls' night, a hospital slumber party of sorts. So, we spent the better part of the evening talking about boys—mostly the two I gave birth to. We painted our nails. We discussed the mission we started together, and it was then that Mom made me promise that I would keep pushing the envelope and scattering (much-needed) love into this crazy world.

"Don't stop," she said. "Keep going, and don't hold onto my love. Give it away ... a little bit every day!"

"I promise."

"As for my stuff," she continued. "I want you to keep my Smith & Wesson .38 Special, my engagement ring and my car; those belong to you. Pack up the rest of it and give it to Goodwill. You don't need it."

"Okay," I whispered, fighting back tears.

Man, this was brutal.

"God's got bigger plans in store for you, Nat," she

continued, her eyes watering. "When He takes something, He always gives you something greater in return."

I couldn't believe this was happening.

"Oh, and I'm going to try and 'hold on' until my social security check clears on the first, so that you have a little buffer."

"Mom, you just said God had bigger plans in store for me."

"He does," she sighed.

"Then don't worry about a buffer. I'm going to be just fine."

At the time, I wasn't sure that was true, but it sounded good—brave. Like me, Mom was talking tough, giving things away and telling her doctors to go fly a kite, but I got the sense she was worried, mostly about leaving me alone, so I joked, "Well, now that you're out of the way, I can *finally* run off with George Clooney!"

I don't know if it was her way of getting back at me for painting her toenails purple and orange, or for being so glib, but she said something that hit me kind of funny.

"Isn't he married?" she asked. "I'm sorry, babe, but I think you're going to be single for a *really long* time."

"Excuse me?" I huffed, shifting my focus from her feet to her face.

"No man is *ever* going to understand you writing random Love Notes to big, strong hero types. That man does not exist."

Are you kidding me?

"Please tell me this is not your deathbed confession," I broached. "I was hoping for something a little more inspiring, like finding out you secretly own a horse ranch up in Montana or you know where Jimmy Hoffa is buried."

"I'm just saying," she replied.

"Are you planning on taking my love life with you," I asked, only half kidding. "Because I don't remember signing the DNR."

We both giggled, but I was devastated because 1.) Mom was rarely wrong, and 2.) People tend to get real on their deathbeds. On top of which, I knew that there was no one that would ever love me the way this woman loved me, and it was beginning to sink in like a lead boot that I might never feel that brand of love again.

When I left the hospital that night, my fingernails painted purple and orange to match Mom's, I was a train wreck. That last little nugget Mom left me with was not enough to interfere with my focus, but it was enough to get under my skin—par for the course. I didn't always like Mom's input, but her remarks stuck with me, nevertheless. They still do, which goes to show, there is no separation of mother and daughter, not even in death. So, what does a girl do when she doesn't want to listen to her mama? She goes straight to her Papa. On the drive home, I whispered a little prayer.

Dear God, my faith is in You!
Thank You that I survive this woman,
and thank You for the good man coming for me.
Please keep him safe in his own battle, so
that he has the strength to find me and love me,
almost as much as You and Mom do.

With that prayer, I pressed two fingers to my lips and blew a kiss up to Heaven. In my mind, I knew for certain there were some really hard days ahead of me, but in my heart, I had faith that it was just as Romans 8:28 was written: *"In all things God works for the good of those who love him and have been called according to his purpose."*

Natalie, thank you so much for your kind note and encouragement. Please keep me in your prayers! God bless you.

—Kristi Noem, Governor of South Dakota

FOURTEEN

Basic Human Need

Mom, the sage that she was, would always say that she would move in any direction, except in reverse. She was very matter of fact about it. I can't tell you how many times she would say, "I don't move backwards."

I think about those words a lot, especially when life takes a hard turn for the worst. Sometimes the easy thing to do is to stand still or retreat back to old habits, even if it no longer makes sense. Pushing forward, as uncomfortable as it can be, is the most fruitful, if not fulfilling response to uncomfortable circumstances.

Fear shrinks—courage advances.

The act, itself, of pushing forward is a boon for a life less ordinary, even if we have to feign courage. And since we only get one shot at an extraordinary life, what have we got to lose?

Only everything we ever dreamed of.

The night Mom died, a part of me died with her. The ache in my heart was almost unbearable, but it was clear to me that I had a decision to make. I could take refuge in my grief, which would be completely understandable, considering the circumstances, or I could push on and live up to the nickname Mom gave me—Gluey.

I was leaning toward the latter.

Being at Mom's bedside, watching her eyes say goodbye to her children and grandchildren and then watching helplessly as she neared her last breath was too much for me to take. I could stomach just about anything, months of cancer treatment, doctors with no bedside manner, cleaning up the effects of chemotherapy from my wood floor, but I could not bear to sit back and watch this woman die. I just didn't have it in me. And, so, when her breathing became shallow and her face gaunt, I stood up abruptly and said something to the effect of, "I'm going home. I'll be back in the morning."

My brother and his wife, Jennifer, looked at me sideways. Their expressions asking, *You're leaving NOW?* They, too, were mentally and emotionally exhausted, but they both seemed to understand my sudden need to take leave. My brother took me into his thick arms and squeezed me tighter than he ever had.

"I love you, Sissy," he said.

In that moment I realized three very important things were happening: 1.) We were losing the matriarch of our family and life, as we knew it, was about to change irreparably, 2.) My heart was crushed and 3.) My little brother and his family had rescued me in the end. Even though I knew Mom hated my younger brother and his family seeing her like that, I needed their help. I couldn't have done any of it without them.

I'm not proud of it, but I ran out of the room with my tail tucked between my legs. I've never been good at goodbye. I am pretty sure I inherited that cowardly trait from my Great Grandpa

Alexander on my dad's side. I was told he was known for his disappearing act in moments leading up to goodbye. Like him, I never did acquire a comfort for it.

Twenty minutes later, halfway home, my brother called to tell me that she was gone. I pulled off to the side of the road to catch my breath and to let it sink in. I couldn't tell if my tears were that of grief or relief—maybe a little bit of both. Nonetheless, it was over. Mom was no longer in pain, and even though cancer gave its worst, it no longer had a hold on either one of us. The thing that had me in some sort of stranglehold was the fear of not following through with what I had promised. In those last days, I saw regret in Mom's eyes. She said as much on several occasions, "I could have done more."

That look of regret scared me even more than death.

I had a television interview scheduled with Arizona PBS early the next morning. A budding, young reporter with ASU's Walter Cronkite School of Journalism was running a story on Love Notes and its recent collaboration with Centennial High School following the Las Vegas mass shooting in October 2017—a few days before Mom died. Students joined our effort, writing more than 1,000 Love Notes for Las Vegas first responders. I considered canceling, but then it occurred to me that scratching the interview would mean moving backwards, retreating, and as Hope's stubborn daughter, that was not an option. I needed to push forward.

Regardless of my puffy, red eyes, I decided to go through with the interview, if for no other reason than to give a well-deserved nod to a senior named Chelsea Opat, who I randomly met at Starbuck's, and who organized Centennial's impressive contribution. Looking back, after having just lost my best friend, I needed a win. In that respect, Love Notes gave me something to run toward, something I loved almost as much as Mom.

This interview turned out to be a blessing in disguise. I never want to say that I could have done more, which is why I continue to pursue this mission with such fierce resolve. I don't want to reach the end of my life and feel as though I hadn't done enough to bring comfort to others, the kind of comfort Mom brought to me. It is such a small thing, but it is something I can do, and I'm kind of good at it. With the company of a kind woman named Nancy, and the generosity of my Godmother Lila, Mom's favorite aunt, I delivered all 1,000 of those Love Notes to first responders in Las Vegas—law enforcement and firefighters alike.

Speaking of firefighters, I am reminded of a few that helped me in my time of need. I was tucking Mom into bed one night at Hospice, a few nights before they moved her to my brother's house. She was taking her time about departing, so we took her home. Mom and I had just finished watching a news story about our Love Note mission on television. We shot it earlier that night at the Peoria Fire Station 195. It was after eleven o'clock at night, and I'll never forget the look on her face when she told me she was proud of me. Those words swelled inside of me. I had never felt more blessed to be her daughter. Once again, she made me promise that I would keep going, pushing the proverbial envelope.

"Stay on the road less traveled," she said, reiterating the words she had written to me in a letter earlier that year.

For her, this was saying a lot, which is why I eventually had those words tattooed on my left forearm, in her handwriting. She would have hated that for two reasons, 1.) She did not approve of tattoos, and 2.) She hated her handwriting.

After kissing Mom on the forehead, and tucking her into bed, baby-burrito style, just as I had tucked my boys in when they were little, I turned off the light in her room and closed the door behind me.

On my way out, I crossed paths with four uniformed firefighters. They were huddled around a small table in the lobby, looking pretty glum. I had heard the Phoenix Fire Department chaplain was occupying the room across the hall from Mom, succumbing to a year-long battle of esophageal cancer. So, I rifled through my purse and pulled out five first responder Love Notes, four for the firefighters and one for the chaplain. They seemed to appreciate the gesture, almost as much as I appreciated the warm, heartfelt conversation with them, albeit short and sweet.

Seeing that I was going home to an empty house, if you don't count the two cats, I found great comfort in leaning on those four fellow humans who, like me, were coming to terms with their grief. I couldn't tell you their names to save my life, but I can tell you that the brief interaction I had with these men was essential to my healing.

Our need for emotional connection drives our behavior, good, bad, and ugly. I think that's what I love most about Love Notes. They satisfy a basic human need for love, which, incidentally, is one of Maslow's Hierarchy of Needs, on top of physiological and safety. Plus, the gesture, itself, is not one-sided. It is reciprocal and it is, indeed, universal.

We *all* know pain and suffering. Heartbreak is a stranger to no one, which in some weird way yokes us all together. So, whether you think you need it or not, or whether you believe someone deserves it or not, we all could use just a little bit of grace, love and understanding. Love Note Ladies are no different. As strong, stubborn and independent as I am, it turns out I needed those things, too. I've never been one to ask for help. Vulnerability has never been my strong suit, but by putting myself out there, and in sharing love in the midst of losing my best friend, I found something I never expected to find—my people.

Natalie, I feel so much love for you in your struggle. You knew your mom was going to die. She was your tribe, picked for you. In that moment, you had no control over what would happen to your mom. You could have given up and chosen despair, anger, or fear, but YOU chose love. You acted, and not knowing it would happen, you chose your tribe. In a sense you handpicked them.

—Rebecca R., High School Teacher

FIFTEEN

The Girl Next Door

Days after Mom died, the doorbell rang. It was a cool afternoon in October. Fall was making its entrance. The cooler weather was fashionably late in Arizona, as usual. Life, as I knew it, had come to some sort of stand still. The days were quiet. The nights were lonely. Even though I was glad for the reprieve, as it gave me a chance to breathe and refocus my energy, I had been left behind.

That's a terrible feeling.

The boys were gone. Mom was long gone. The house had never felt so empty. I had never felt so useless and alone. It was just me, my two tuxedo cats (Danni and Bella) and a refrigerator on the brink of death. If not for several homecooked plates of food being delivered from friends, neighbors and former Love Note recipients, I might have fell through the cracks altogether.

The doorbell rang a second time. When I opened the front door, I found Nyanna, a beautiful blonde-haired girl with big, blue-green eyes. She was my next-door neighbor, a nine-year-old twig with long limbs and a purposeful smile. She stood determined on my doormat, as if she had good reason to be there. I thought maybe she was looking for a lost dog or selling candy bars for school, but it was more than that.

"Do you want to hang out?" she asked.

I looked over her shoulder, expecting to see her mom or her brothers playing out front. There was nobody. It was just her.

"Does your mom know you're here?"

"I think so," she smiled. "Can we do something?"

She seemed awfully eager. It wasn't like I had a lot going on that day, so I chewed on it for a second. Nyanna crossed her fingers and her knees for luck, closing her eyes tight, as if that would help her chances of getting in the door. I couldn't imagine why, all of a sudden, this girl wanted to hang out with me, the soon-to-be cat lady on the corner lot. I mean, it wasn't like she and I had ever hung out together in the past. Except for standing out front, talking with her mom, while she and her siblings ran circles around us, we had never spent time together.

This was a first.

"Please, please, pleeeeeease ..." she begged.

"Only if you go tell your mom that you are here," I replied.

"Yes," she exclaimed, shooting off like a bottle rocket back to her house. I barely had time to close the door and sit back down on the couch before the doorbell rang for the third time. It was Nyanna. I could smell the burning rubber from her Keds®.

I held the door open, as she pushed past me, making her way into the kitchen. You would have thought I was throwing a party for the last living unicorn or something. The girl was *that* excited. Just then I got a text message. It was Nyanna's mom—Tiffany. She wrote: *"Thanks for having her, but please send her home, if she becomes a nuisance."*

I reassured Tiffany that we would be fine, and we were. Nyanna and I hung out, made food and talked about girl stuff, an experience foreign to me, being the mother of boys. I wasn't expecting company that day, but it felt good to have someone to talk to and laugh with about silly, not-so-serious stuff.

After a couple of hours, and as many ibuprofen, I walked Nyanna home, feeling a renewed sense of energy, not to mention exhaustion. She wrapped her gangly arms around me, giving me the tightest, most heartfelt squeeze. It was just what the doctor ordered.

Over the next several months, my doorbell rang nearly every day, sometimes several times a day and sometimes as early as six o'clock in the morning. It was always Nyanna, raring to go. She was determined to hang out with me, so determined, in fact, that her mother started referring to her as "Nyanna the Stalker." She would send text messages to me that read: *"I am so, so sorry that she is stalking you. I don't know what has gotten into her."*

The truth is Nyanna was a breath of fresh air. She became my buddy in just about everything—shopping, Starbuck's, cooking, baking, delivering Love Notes. She and I made trips across the Valley, visiting police departments and fire stations. She was a real trooper! I think our time together made her feel special, riding on big, red rigs with firefighters and eating glazed donuts with cops. We had the most fun together, and I can't say I would have been as ambitious to deliver so much love at that time, had it not been for her. She was a godsend, not to mention severely allergic to my cats. The poor thing's eyes would get red and puffy. And yet she persisted in showing up. I was beginning to wonder if I wasn't Nyanna's version of a "mama goat" in the grand scheme of things.

One day in December, I made the mistake of telling Nyanna that I wasn't in the mood to put up my Christmas tree.

"I usually put it up on Thanksgiving night," I said. "Somewhere in between leftovers and Black Friday."

Nyanna sprang to her feet, and in fairy-like fashion, she put her hands on her hips, threw her chin up into the air and said, "It's Christmas! We're putting up your tree right now, missy!"

I half expected her to fly around the room, waving a wand and sprinkling pixie dust. I sank deeper into the couch, shaking my head. It was the first time in forever that I wasn't feeling it, that deep craving for Christmas. Too much had happened. Too much had been lost. I was tired, perhaps even unwilling to let the spirit of the holiday get the better of me.

Besides, it was just me in that house. Where is the fun in that? The thing that always made constructing Christmas exciting was the people around me, the magic I saw reflected in their eyes. It was all for their benefit ... or so I thought.

"Where is it?" Nyanna demanded, peeking in closets and bedrooms. "Where is the Christmas tree?"

"Nyanna," I begged. "Not today."

"Get up," she huffed. "Go get the tree!"

Hmmm ... where had I heard that before?

I could see in her eyes that she wasn't about to let this go. It was in that moment (and in that demanding tone) that I felt God may have a hand in all of this, in this nine-year-old girl landing on my doorstep with such fierce determination and a desire to keep me from curling up into a ball and disappearing. Seriously, why did she care so much?

Could it be kismet?

At her command, I pulled the Christmas tree down out of the attic, the very Christmas tree I had assembled for more than a decade in front of the same picture window in my living room. I loved that tree with all my heart. It represented so many fond Christmas memories. Mom found it at a garage sale down the street, practically brand new.

For a fake tree, it was full, faithful and life-like—even after all those years. She paid ten dollars cash for it on a hot July morning. I'll never forget Mom bursting into my bedroom, the one day I opted out of going garage-sale shopping with her. I was hoping to sleep in for once.

"You'll never guess what I found," Mom shrieked. "*The*

most beautiful Christmas tree **ever**, and I only paid ten dollars!"

If my eyes had been open, I would have rolled them.

"You have to come with me to pick it up," she insisted. "It doesn't fit in my car."

Mom was so excited, bound and determined to get me out of bed that morning. God, she loved to push me.

I never thought I would miss that, but I do.

"Seriously, Mom," I exclaimed. "It's seven o'clock, and how beautiful can it be if you only paid ten dollars for it?"

She was killing me.

"Get up," she huffed. "Go get the tree!"

The similarity between Mom and Nyanna's pushiness was uncanny. I was beginning to wonder if Nyanna wasn't sent directly to me by my mother, as she (on more than one occasion) said stuff to me that only my mother would say, like "I like you better *without* the scrunchie in your hair."

Yes. That happened.

That day in December, Nyanna and I put up my Christmas tree, and despite my resistance in the beginning, I let the spirit of the holiday sink in, and it felt good. Over the next couple of days, she and I made Christmas cookies, painted our nails red and green and purchased a brand-new refrigerator.

And every time Kelsea Ballerini's song "Legends" would play on the car radio, she would belt out the chorus with a big smile on her face. It was hard not to be deliriously happy around her. Her friendship yanked me out of my holiday funk. It still brings a smile to my face. For me, her friendship was like a big gulp of hot chocolate on a cold, winter day. It warms you from the inside out, leaving a melted marshmallow mustache under your nose.

Nyanna was my angel, my Christmas angel, albeit a bit on the pushy side. She was a heavenly go between, sent to me from somewhere up above. You'll never convince me otherwise, which makes her a notable part of my love story and a friend for life.

Nyanna and I bundled up and ventured out to Starbuck's later that evening to celebrate our great Christmas-tree conquest. We drank hot chocolate until our bellies ached and devoured frosted, snowman sugar cookies and cake pops like they were going out of style. In our minds, we were just like Kelsea Ballerini's song *Legends*. She and I were legends, and we were writing our own story!

I thank God every day that angel came knocking on my front door. Moreover, I am so glad that I let her in because she found her way straight to my heart, fairly forcibly, I might add.

It's all a part of her charm.

Yes, she was, as her mother put it, something of "stalker," but to me, I'll always remember her as the girl who saved Christmas.

I love you, Nyanna! Stay just as you are.

Thank you so much for all of the cards. Your efforts are appreciated and comes at a time when our firefighters, EMTs and paramedics need this type of support. I find it amazing that people from a location so far from Dayton will take time out of their day to support us and encourage us to continue our mission. Thank you for these notes and for all you do.

—Jeff Payne, Fire Chief, Dayton Fire Department

SIXTEEN

Christmas in New York

While we're on the subject of angels, there were a few deployed that year to help get me through the holidays, which leads me to believe that there is something to this kindness thing. Miracles are born from it. I have witnessed it.

When Mom was in Hospice, a long, lost cousin named Debbie showed up from out of the blue. She had flown in from a small town in New Mexico. She heard that Mom was dying, and she wanted to say goodbye. I had only met Debbie once when I was a baby. Hence, I had no recollection of her. However, I was so moved that she showed up and so was Mom.

When Debbie arrived on scene, we clicked almost instantly. It was as if we had always known each other. Having her around, along with my Godmother Lila and my cousin Bernadine, was a godsend. I needed to be surrounded by the women in my tribe. Like Mom, they are very much a part of the fabric of who I am. I will always be grateful to have had them close in those last days of Mom's life.

After Mom passed away, Debbie and I talked on the telephone quite a bit. We'd go on for hours, like old friends. When she asked what was next for me, I mentioned that I had always dreamed of visiting Rockefeller Center in New York City at Christmas. Standing beneath that big, beautiful Christmas tree was at the top of my bucket list. Debbie, being the giver that she is, wasted no time in making that happen.

A few weeks before Christmas, she bought me a roundtrip plane ticket to New York and reserved a hotel room in Midtown Manhattan with a dazzling view of the Empire State Building.

Her thoughtfulness still makes me want to cry.

I spent a couple of days tooling around New York City, taking in the twinkling lights, the Christmas tree at Rockefeller Center, the bundled-up skaters holding hands as they circled the ice rink, the Saks Fifth Avenue Holiday Light Show and the Christmas carolers in Time Square.

It was magical, but even more than that, it was medicinal—food for the soul. I was all by myself on this urban expedition, and in a way, it was the fresh start I needed.

Of course, it was also freezing cold, but I had on my Cuddle Duds, the best brand of long underwear—EVER! I also had a big bundle of Love Notes stuffed in my backpack, which also kept me warm. I don't think I  would have survived the cold without those two things.

It just so happened to be the week President Trump was

coming to town. Therefore, the city streets were all buttoned down with road barriers and cops on every corner. The entrance to Trump Plaza had secret service agents on the ready, armed with semi-automatic rifles. On one hand, it was like shooting fish in a barrel when it came to distributing Love Notes. There were NYPD officers everywhere.

On the other hand, it made it difficult to navigate the city on the morning of his arrival. I couldn't even cross the street to get back to my hotel until his motorcade  passed. While it was kind of a mess, it was actually quite cool getting to see the President of the United States, even if he was just driving past. I got goosebumps when I saw the impressive, long line of motor cops with flashing red and blue lights coming toward me and a handful of black sedans and limousines following from behind.

I mean, how often does that happen?

I thought about Mom and how much she would have loved to witness all of this. At the same time, I could just see her shaking her head, thinking to herself, *How shameless is my daughter?*

I stood smiling at the edge of an empty sidewalk, holding a warm cup of hot chocolate and waving as President Trump drove by. The sedan windows were blackened, but I waved just the same.

Life is crazy, isn't it? You just never know where you'll end up.

The world belongs to the shameless.

I spent the better part of two days, and a good portion of two nights, meandering around the city. I delivered Love Notes to so many on-duty NYPD police officers, including the mounted unit in the heart of Central Park. I was cleaning up! There were first responders everywhere. God love New York City! I delivered Love Notes to a few FDNY fire houses, NYPD sub stations and even Penn Station. I left Love Notes on police cars, veteran cars and subway cars.

It was great!

On my last night in the Big Apple, I was determined to find a real pizza joint and get a couple of authentic slices of New-York style pizza. One would think it would be easy, but I pounded the pavement until my feet hurt and my blood sugar had dropped so low that I thought I might have to settle for the golden arches across the street—not my favorite! I finally found a joint. It was somewhere off the main grid. The street was skinny and dark, and I was sure that I would be mugged and/or murdered before I made it to the end of the street where the word "PIZZA" glowed in bright, red lights.

Again, somewhere Mom was shaking her head.

When I returned to my hotel room, I sat on the small sofa next to the window and demolished two delicious slices of pepperoni pizza the size of my suitcase. The Empire State Building kept me company. It sparkled, winking at me with its red and green lights. I held my thumb up to the window, positioning it over the 1,454-foot structure, making the famed skyscraper disappear (and reappear) in the cityscape.

It was magic—all of it.

It was also close to midnight, and the city was still stirring. Taxi horns were blowing. People the size of ants were milling up and down the sidewalks. It reminded me of Washington DC, those nights spent snuggled up to the hotel window, eavesdropping on the city. It made me miss Mom. My heart literally ached for her. I wanted to talk with her, tell her all about my day—the Love Notes, President Trump, the interactions with strangers. She would have loved all of it, but she would have been none too happy that I was walking the streets of New York alone in the middle of the night, the "murder capital of the world" in her mind, wandering aimlessly down blind alleys looking for pizza. However, as much as she worried about me, she would have been so happy to know that I was still at it. In one of her last letters to me, she wrote, *"Stay on the road less traveled and suddenly you will come upon your treasure."*

Mom would not have wanted me to shrink into the shadows. She would have wanted me to move courageously ahead with my life, any direction but backwards.

One of the most fun Love Note deliveries I make is on commercial airliners. When I board an airplane, I hand out six Love Notes, all of which are tied neatly together with a pretty ribbon, making one big bundle. I address one note to the captain, one to the first mate and four to the flight crew. The reaction is immediate. I am always met with toothy smiles, and the exuberant, "That is so sweet, Ma'am! What row are you seated?"

Delivering the unexpected instantly separates you from the herd, which is kind of a neat feeling. Everyone wants to feel special, which is why the small gesture makes such a profound impact to both the recipient *and* to the bearer.

I travel across the country quite a bit. In the past few years, I have flown to and from New York, Chicago, Cleveland, Dallas, Phoenix, Norfolk, Spokane, Las Vegas and San Diego. I've taken many of these trips more than once. And in that time, I have delivered Love Notes to flight crews.

In return, I have been called out by captains over the

intercom. I've been invited up to the cockpit for conversation and selfies. Flight attendants have gushed, cried and even spoiled me with plastic captain's wings, cookies, snacks, big bottles of wine, miniature bottles of champagne, overnight kits that include socks, sewing kits and satin sleep masks. I've even been promoted to First Class. I tell you this, not to impress you, but rather to inspire you.

When we stop concerning ourselves with our own comfort, seeking out reasons to be incensed with how poorly people treat us, and start focusing on how we can bring comfort to others and treat them better, the game changes. People want to be good to you when you are good to them.

It's that simple.

On a flight home from Dallas, I handed the flight crew a bundle of six Love Notes, one for each. It's always fun to watch their faces light up, turn from confusion to sunshine in the breadth of time it takes to say, "These are for you."

After reading her Love Note, one flight attendant found me and said, "I checked the manifest and you are in the wrong seat."

I was squished (two deep) in the window seat, like a sardine. I looked at her funny and was about to check my boarding pass when she winked at me.

"Oh," I smiled, catching on. "Silly me!"

That inspired flight attendant moved me to an empty row with all the leg room in the world.

Manifest, indeed.

We do get what we give, not to mention what we focus on.

"Thank you," I said.

She leaned in and whispered, "*You* made our day!"

That, in a nutshell, is what it's all about!

It's not about the airline swag. It's about the smiles, the conversation, the reciprocation of gratitude. I don't always accept the gifts I mentioned above. That's not what this mission is about. This mission is about making people feel loved. In doing so, you can't help but to feel loved in return, even if all you get back is a smile. You have no idea the power of small kindnesses.

It is life changing.

On top of which, that spirit of generosity is contagious.

And that is a good thing.

At a time when politicians and the media are hellbent on dividing our nation, creating angst, hatred and fear in our homes, in our city streets, at our schoolboard meetings and even 30,000 feet up in the air, it's no wonder people are so profoundly moved by the simplest show of love.

Gratitude changes everything!

Natalie, in a world where more and more people are thinking of nothing but themselves, you are thinking about nothing but love. I felt so special when I received your note. You are creating powerful and memorable moments in peoples' lives. Thank you for the time you take to spread love like fire.

—Ryan Rodriquez, Firefighter/Paramedic

SEVENTEEN

Reinforcements

I f you're like me, someone who believes that everything happens for a reason, you must also assume the same is true of everyone. Whether it is for a lifetime, a life lesson, or a simple plot twist devised to steer you into an unexpected direction, I believe people come into our life for good reason, whether we know what that reason is or not. Because of a Love Note, so many good people have come into my life, including a woman who I'll call Jane. Now, Jane isn't someone I would catalogue as a "girlfriend," per se, but she is a kind soul who I connected with during my role-playing days with Elise and our local law enforcement.

While she and I never met outside of scenario-based training for lunch, or shopping, or to bare our souls over cappuccinos, we did have a shared love for our community and for those who keep it safe. As we would come to find, neither Jane nor I have a problem with large, tact-out SWAT officers coming at us barrel first, shouting, "Show me your hands!"

But put me in the path of a runaway June bug, and I come unglued.

Jane is a notable part of my love story. I'm not sure she knows that. She is a real sweetheart, a good, church-going gal who kept me in cardstock and who, as it turned out, introduced me to one of the of *the* most compelling chapters of this story.

It all started rather innocently, as things do. One day, in between training scenarios, we role players were standing around chewing the fat. Training days can go long, so there was a lot of down time for us to catch up on girl talk.

"I met this really great guy," Jane gushed. "His name is Chris. He's a retired street cop who has an unbelievable story of survival. He's writing a book about his twenty-year career in law enforcement and the gunfight that changed his life. I really need to introduce the two of you. Maybe you can help him publish it."

As a freelance writer and editor, she had my attention. The way she went on about this guy, I got the feeling his story was pretty important to the law-enforcement community. I also got the feeling there was something more going on between he and Jane. She seemed awfully giddy every time she spoke of him.

"I'd love to meet him," I replied. "It could be something!"

Chris sounded like a great catch, professionally speaking. However, months passed, and Jane never did put me in touch with this storied street cop. I had a hunch she wanted to keep him for herself. She continued to rave about him at trainings, telling us girls about how the two of them had been spending time together. Jane was obviously into this guy. At least, that was the rumor mill. I didn't ask questions. Outside of this man's manuscript, and the fact that he had been involved in something rather significant in his career, the rest of the story was nothing more than scuttlebutt.

Speaking of "scuttlebutts," we were getting ours handed to

us by SWAT in these trainings. Not that we were complaining.

We knew going in that these training events were designed for realism, so it could get a little intense, to say the least. The business of "protecting and serving" is not for the faint of heart, so the  scenarios and the language can be a little salty, to say nothing of the Simunition rounds.

Being the mother of a sailor and (now) a Texas deputy, I show up to these trainings with thicker skin than most. My willingness to take part is threefold: 1.) A part of me has always been curious about a career in uniform, 2.) Short of jumping out of an airplane, a little adrenaline boost is good for the soul, and 3.) I was just so happy to be there, a million miles away from sitting at my mother's bedside at Hospice. Seriously, it was all I could do to keep from smiling, as I helped act out training scenarios, even when being (forcefully) taken into "custody."

One of my favorite parts of these trainings is at the end of the day when the words "end scenario" reverberate throughout the building and our protective gear comes off. The officers carefully pat us down, looking for the effects of marking cartridges (i.e., bullet holes). With much concern, they ask, "You good?"

Yeah, I'm good.

The truth is, save a few bumps and bruises here and there, I couldn't be better. The reason being, Elise, Jane and those law enforcement officers were like guardian angels. They were my reinforcements. Their presence in those dark days was a substantial part of my healing. There is no way these good men and women could possibly know just how much they have meant to me. Even now, as I write this, it is hard to put into words, except to say that had it not been for them, and for those SWAT trainings that pushed me out of my comfort zone, I don't know where I'd be today.

They rescued me for real, and they didn't even know it.

I think back to those days when the pain of losing Mom was fresh. Showing up to those training events kept my courage in check. It kept my head on straight. It gave me something that I wouldn't have found anywhere else—the guts to keep on going.

Plus, it put me up close and personal with those heroes who put it all on the line for their community, the ones I was writing to every day. And, in doing so, it put me in a position to give them something they don't get a lot of these days—love and gratitude. In return, I was magnetically drawn to the people and the places I belong. That's the beauty of it. It's like Rumi, the thirteen-century Persian poet, said, "What you seek is seeking you."

*I received a note from you a couple of days before Thanksgiving …
That note really made my day. I had lost my father earlier in the
year and my mother was in hospice care and was told that day she
was not going to be much longer. Your card helped me through the
day. As a veteran and law enforcement officer, I thank you for the
card. It is a wonderful thing you are doing!*

—Charles M., Veteran/Law Enforcement Officer

EIGHTEEN
Blue Notes

I am told that in music, it's the blue notes that create the heart-wrenching tones that move people to tears. In the case of Love Notes, it's the "Blue Notes" that bring me to tears. As a mom to a Texas deputy, you could say that I have a soft spot for our nation's law enforcement.

You know who you are!

You are the badge-carrying, tact-out hero who (on the outside!) is about as soft and cuddly as a heavy-duty toolbox, but whose insides are nothing but teddy bear stuffing and maple syrup. Seriously! You guys are the sweetest, but don't worry. Your secret is safe with me.

I'm a lucky girl in that the law enforcement family—blood and blue—welcomed me into their tight-knit circle with open arms. I know that's no easy feat. Of all the heroes I've approached, and there have been many, it's the LEO that gave me serious pause. Because of their tough exterior, I let many of them get away. That is to say, I was too timid to approach them with a Love Note. It wasn't the fact that they carried a firearm and taser. That's not what worried me. It was how they carried themselves. Behind those dark sunglasses and "do not come hither" stare, I was forced out of my shell when it came to hand delivering gratitude to this brand of hero.

With their full-on stance and their thumbs purposefully pushed into the arm pit of their Kevlar vests, I consistently found myself questioning whether or not a Love Note was even necessary. On the surface of things, these warriors project confidence

like none other. They are poised to protect at all costs, no matter the violence that awaits them. Come to find these particular protectors, above them all, were the most grateful for the show of love. Because they dare not let on how much they hurt on any given day, it was their consolation and comradery that I least expected.

A couple of years into my mission, I was invited to attend a squad briefing just before embarking on a police ride along—one of eight that I've completed in the state of Arizona. Just before dismissing the squad, the sergeant introduced me to his team.

"Hey! By the way, this is Natalie," he barked. "She writes these *little* love notes."

The briefing room rippled with amusement, making me feel somewhat silly.

Little love notes—indeed!

That was my cue to buck up and, so I reached into my purse, pulled out a small bundle of Love Notes and personally

132

handed one to each of the officers. Silly or not, I was on a mission. I was thanking them and that was that.

Super gluey ... remember.

Later that day, the officer I was riding with parked beneath a giant, shade tree, so she could write some reports. The sergeant from the morning briefing edged up next to us in his patrol car. He rolled down his window, and I rolled mine down in kind. The sergeant sighed, resting his arm on the door panel. After a few minutes of small talk, he got a toothy grin and said, "Natalie, I want to show you something."

He tugged at his sun visor. Out slipped a Love Note with the words, "Thank you, Officer!" handwritten on the envelope in *my* handwriting. The sergeant held it up to his face, and with thick, pinkened fingers pinching the note, he said with watery eyes, "You left this on my car a couple of years ago. I read it after the really rough calls. It helps."

I smiled, biting my bottom lip to keep from crying.

I needed that!

On those days when I question if what I'm doing is making a difference, I think back to that afternoon under the giant, shade tree. I think about that sergeant and his Love Note that remains tucked up under his sun visor. It reminds me of something Mahatma Gandhi said, *"Whatever you do will be insignificant, but it is very important that you do it."*

Something tells me that this is what he meant by that. So, if in doubt, just do something nice for someone. You will never know who needs that small gesture of grace. Believe me when I say, it's the little things that mean the most. And, on a side note, for you law enforcement officers out there, it's not the badge that makes you our hero. It's the heart behind it! We see you.

I got the note you left on my patrol car ... I can't tell you what it means to have gotten this today. This note is something I will cherish. It's things like this that help me through the days with rough calls ... I look at it daily at the start of my shift. I had a long few days last week, and I can't begin to tell you how it helps me. I've been following your page since I received your note, and it makes me smile daily. The positive energy you radiate is something that I think the world could use more of. Thank you so much, Natalie! If you ever want to venture out to Buckeye, let me know!

—Sgt. Zach Astrup, Law Enforcement Officer

NINETEEN

Day of the Dumpster

Mom would have been so mad at me, agreeing to meet a perfect stranger next to a big, ugly, green dumpster behind a Walgreen's out in the middle of nowhere. I can hear her now, "You are *way* too trusting, Nat!"

I was embarking upon unfamiliar territory. I, Hope's only daughter, was foolishly playing with fire (again!), living out a scene one might read in a James Patterson novel. You know the one, the one where the ditzy broad walks into a blind alley, straight into the hands of a serial killer while attempting to deliver a Love Note to a complete stranger. I can hear the news headline now: *Love Note Lady Discovered Dead in Dumpster, Film at Eleven.*

Did it stop me?

Heck no!

Some things never change. I am eternally middle school's "Biggest Dreamer," the dogged idealist chasing that allusive rabbit down a hole. Most wouldn't bother, but like Alice, I have come to realize that it is often life's "rabbit holes" that lead us to our Wonderland—our destiny.

I literally drove more than forty miles (one way!) to the outskirts of nowhere—Buckeye, Arizona, to be exact. We're talking the serial killer's dream spot for discarding bodies. I am certain most ruthless killers follow the same three golden rules of real estate—Location. Location. Location.

It was the last day in January 2019. The "stranger" had reached out six months earlier, having received one of my Love Notes on his patrol vehicle at a police training event. I really had no other reason to drive out to Buckeye, except to make the connection. Don't think that it didn't occur to me that meeting a perfect stranger in such a precarious place might be a terrible idea. I mean, this guy's profile photo on Facebook pictured him wearing a Deadpool costume, lending no identifiable facial features to positively ID him in a lineup. On messenger, he said he was a "cop" and a "Love Note recipient." I took his word for it.

Too trusting—I know, Mother!

Because I was committed to pushing the proverbial envelope (along with the real thing), I went against my better judgement, as well as Mom's and ventured out to meet this "cop."

Somewhere Mom is still shaking her head.

I tend to give people the benefit of the doubt. Considering the level of crazy running rampant in the world today, some may deem this as a chink in my armor, but if I'm being perfectly honest, it's one of my favorite things about me. Years ago, I worked for a really great guy named Victor, and he gave me one of the best compliments I've ever been given. He said, "Natalie, don't take this the wrong way, but your disposition is very childlike. I don't mean childish. What I mean to say is you are so pure and uncomplicated.

You still believe the best in people."

I love that. Does it make me too trusting?

Totally.

Mom made no bones about her displeasure in my trusting nature and risk-taking behavior. This, coming from the woman who (twice!) randomly picked up roadside strangers to give them a much-needed lift. As usual, I took her critique with a grain of salt.

The first of her random passengers was a young, black woman she spotted walking in the heat of summer in Arizona. It turned out, the woman was on her way to the veterinarian, lugging a large pet carrier containing her sick cat. The woman had a few miles left to go. In case you didn't know, Arizona summers are deadly, so Mom might have saved a life (or two!) that day.

The second of her roadside rescues was an older woman who had missed the bus to work. Both times Mom pulled over and offered these women a ride, and both times the women revered her as their "guardian angel," which leads me to believe that my blind faith in people is not entirely arbitrary, but rather something handed down to me, an heirloom of sorts. I think Mom conveniently forgot whose example I was led by.

Do as I say, not as I do. Right, Ma?

In her defense, she did teach me to be ever aware of my surroundings. Days before she died, she reminded me to "keep my eyes peeled in parking lots." I am positive that advice has saved my skin on more than one occasion. While I am trusting of people, I'm no easy mark. I'm just every bit the apple that fell from Hope's tree, which makes me every bit my mother's daughter. I am also quite stubborn and headstrong, traits I also inherited from her.

That said, I count my lucky stars that I didn't cross paths with a serial killer that day at the dumpster. Instead, "Deadpool" turned out to be a sergeant with the Buckeye Police Department. His name is Zach. I found him just as he said I would, with his patrol vehicle backed into a parking space behind the Walgreen's. He was right next to the big, ugly, green dumpster. My heart was racing, as I pulled into the parking space next to him. There was slight consolation (for both of us) in that it was broad daylight, and the dumpster in question was visible from a major intersection, no more than eighty yards away.

Thank God for small favors.

As I rolled up on scene, turned off my engine and pushed open my car door, a tall shadow fell over me. It was the sergeant. He was standing between me and the face of the sun. He wasted no time reaching out his hand to introduce himself and to thank me, once more, for the Love Note. He seemed somewhat nervous. As I looked up at him, my eyes squinting in the sunlight, I remember thinking to myself, *This dude is a giant!* With all the gear (i.e.,

Kevlar vest, gun belt, gun, taser, badge, stereo-typical dark sunglasses, kitchen sink), he was reminiscent of the Terminator.

That is ... until he spoke.

There was something so genuine about this officer. He spoke so candidly, which isn't characteristic of most cops. Most hold their emotions close to their vest. I didn't want to stare, but I couldn't help but notice his lip was quivering as he thanked me, and even though I couldn't see his eyes for the black Oakley's, I would have bet my life they were wet.

This wasn't my first rodeo.

Although, it was *the* first cop I made (ahem!) cry.

Sorry, Sarge!

If you were to ask him, the sergeant would tell you that someone must have been cutting onions nearby or that the pollen count was high that day, but the truth is, he was moved. Zach was not the first to let down his guard because of a Love Note, and I doubt very highly that he will be the last. It was a small miracle that we met that day. I will never take for granted those tender moments between two strangers. I think that's what I wish the most from this mission, that people see how effortless it is to connect with a stranger at a human level—no matter how different we appear on skin surface.

Zach shared how he was suspicious of the Love Note at first because, just one week prior, an all-points bulletin had gone out to law enforcement across the country. The memo warned officers that groups of individuals were lacing flyers with fentanyl and then purposely placing them under windshield wipers of police vehicles.

He had just finished an all-day training event and wasn't quite sure how to handle the "suspicious" envelope tucked beneath the windshield wiper of his Tahoe. He had a few options: 1.) He could put on a pair of protective gloves before handling it, 2.) He could deploy the windshield wiper until the note fell off and let the wind take it or 3.) He could simply take the risk in opening it.

Zach opted for option three, risk opening the Love Note. And I am so glad he did.

"I figured there were enough firefighters on our training site to resuscitate me, if it came to that," he laughed.

Curiosity always gets the cat ... and sometimes the cop.

Zach and I had a good laugh that day. As a matter of fact, the "day of the dumpster" has become something of an inside joke between us. I guess that's better than a gnarly headline.

Right?

Just before parting ways, Zach (who is also an Air Force reservist), gave me a challenge coin and an open invite to ride along with the Buckeye Police Department. On that note, he sent me off with a great, big bear hug that nearly crushed my cheekbone against the steel cage protecting his chest.

Owie!

It's not always easy to see with our law enforcement officers, but somewhere beneath that tough, outer exterior, beats the human heart of a hero. Underneath the steel plates, weapon system and cynical disposition, lives a flesh and bone human being.

Personally, I am convinced they are the best and the bravest of us!

I love them so much!

These days, cops get a bad rap, but if not them, who is going to bring down the hammer on crime? Firefighters put out fires. Cops catch bad guys. Both are desperately needed in our community. Therefore, both deserve all the love we can give them because the work they do is not easy. Loving our firefighters, however, is easy. Cops, on the other hand, take a little more time warming up to, but once you get them … you've got them for good!

Since that day at the dumpster, Zach has made many trips with me and the gang to speak to businesses and schools about the power of gratitude and how a simple act of kindness can (and will) defeat adversity. His story has become an important part of our love story, and he has become one of my all-time best friends. I could cry when I think of all the good people who have come into my life since losing Mom.

Damn the pollen!

The better part of this mission is about fostering love and gratefulness. We have so much to be thankful for in this country, beginning with our nation's heroes. However, don't say the word "hero" too loud. These brave men and women will deny it, claiming that they are "just doing their job." Our veterans and first responders carry a heavy burden, and I don't take that for granted.

Even though the gesture, itself, is random and simplistic in nature, and oftentimes anonymous, I want people to know that these Love Notes are no accident. It is all by design. I also would like to state for the record that I am so happy, if not somewhat relieved that my love story did not end at the dumpster that day. I have a lot of work yet to do before the words, "and she was never seen again" are written about me.

Thank you for being a friend, Zach!

Natalie, not many people we know have found the purpose for their life. Not only have you found yours; it aligns with His purpose for us. Thank you so much for listening to that inner voice and spreading love to those in need. May God continue to bless you and your mission.

—Alan & Linda, P.,
Law Enforcement Officer (RET).

TWENTY

A Magnet for Miracles

I t's funny, but the more Love Notes I write, the more I come to understand and appreciate the Law of Attraction. It's true what they say. What you put into this world has no choice but to return to you, tenfold. This mission was never meant to be about anything more than getting Mom out of bed and sparking love in our community. However, it instantly became so much more because, as has been proven, time and time again, you get what you give in this life.

The more handwritten love and inspiration I deliver to strangers, the more these so-called "strangers" give back to me. Whether they simply share their story or they break down into tears, there is a level of trust they put in me, and I don't take that for granted. The truth is we humans are not so different that we can't find consolation in one another, even in the short time it takes to order a cup of coffee. If all we have to offer someone is a reassuring smile, we will have created a ripple effect of love. To be of any benefit to humanity, one must first be open to the notion that we are all imperfect and that the guy standing in line in front of you, no matter his political affiliation or walk of life, is as deserving of love and kindness as the gal standing in front of him. It is not our job to pick and choose who we feel is deserving of love and who is not. That mindset gets us nowhere. Besides, the world has enough "Karen's." The true miracle begins when we simply give love and understanding for the sake of giving, in any given situation.

I spent the better part of five years investing my time, love, money, and energy in doing just that—giving love away. And I would do it all over again because it exposed (and exponentially increased) my superpower. Would you like to know what that superpower is?

Come close ... closer.

It is **gratitude**, my friend. A grateful life is a fulfilled life. It is as easy and elementary as it sounds. Gratitude is not forced or manipulated. It is thankfulness—pure and simple. It is waking up every day and finding *one thing* to be thankful for, no matter how much money is in your bank account or whether or not you are in perfect health. It must be practiced every single day, even when you don't feel like it. This is where it gets sticky because God knows we don't always feel like it, especially when it comes to showing gratitude to strangers. Most of the time we blow off steam on people we don't know. For instance, if we don't agree with someone or we don't know them from Adam, we tend to hold out, save our love and gratitude for those who are most like us. But what about the stranger standing in line behind you at the coffee shop or at the grocery store? Do we *not* show them love and gratitude because we don't know who they are, where they came from or who they voted for?

Does any of that even matter?

John 13:34 reads: *"Love one another, as I have loved you."* It could be the police officer who just pulled the lifeless baby out of an algae-ridden swimming pool, or the firefighter who suffered smoke inhalation while rescuing the family dog from a burning house. It could be the war veteran who lost a leg in combat, or worse, a best friend. It could be the nurse who is coming off a 24-hour shift with no sleep or a young, single mother working two jobs while raising a handful of small children. Moreover, it could be you coming off a bad week, which leads me to the question: Who among us doesn't deserve a little love and gratitude on *any* given day?

Believe me when I say, even the slightest acknowledgement between humans can be lifesaving, creating a ripple effect—a smile, a compliment, a kind word, a handshake, a hug, a thank you, a complimentary cup of coffee, a Love Note. Our faith in humanity, our confidence in ourselves, our health, and happiness feed off such simple kindnesses. And it doesn't have to cost a thing. I love the way Jim Carrey puts it. He said, *"The effect you have on others is the most valuable currency there is."*

That's God's honest truth, friends!

I was one of the lucky ones. My mom was great at feeding her children and grandchildren kind words, hugs and smiles, even if we didn't think we needed it and, more importantly, when we didn't deserve it. Mom was never the touchy-feely type, far from it, and yet she was always there with hugs, humor and hope, particularly when the chips were down. With the same token, she was real with us when we needed her to be. Being real with people was her strong suit. I suppose losing her and that intrinsic vote of confidence and honesty is what motivates me today because *that* brand of love is what the world needs now. It is desperate for the smallest, realest (most heartfelt) show of love, kindness and truth. These Love Notes are modest, but they are mighty. And they have inspired others across the country to pick up their pens and carry on Mom's legacy. I can't tell you how much that means to me, and how much good has returned to me because of it.

Since Mom became ill, I struggled in just about every way a human can—mentally, spiritually, emotionally, and financially. I was heartbroken, and I was broke. I was just trying to keep my head above water. To make matters worse, I was substitute teaching middle school and high school, barely making ends meet and trying not to succumb to teenage angst. Seriously, my classrooms made SWAT training look like Sesame Street. The students were tough on me, testing my resolve and doing their best to break me. I fought back with my heart. I utilized my Love Note story (and what little gumption I had left) to break down the walls between them and me, to soften the edges and it worked. I opened up about my Love Note adventures, sharing stories of its miracles, and my students ate it up!

The truth is, I wasn't sure where my life was going. The thing that changed everything was gratitude. Rather than focus on my lack, I concentrated on all the good things I had going for me, the stuff I was grateful for—family, friendship, health, a roof over my head, cats curled up at my feet and the ink it took to continue what Mom and I started. In that regard, I had everything I needed. I trusted God to take care of the rest, and He did not disappoint.

Over the years I have asked God for many things, not the least of which was the love of a good man. I've come to believe that you don't need to know *how* a thing will happen, not half as much as you need to have the faith to *know* that it will. If I could ask the Universe for a paperclip and have one land at my feet within minutes, perhaps I could ask for something more noteworthy, like an epic love story. And, so, I prayed on it—every day via knee mail.

Dear God,
Thank You for the good,
strong and courageous man who is coming for me,
the man who will love me for the rest of my days,
almost as much as You love me.
Deliver him safely.
Amen.

I repeated those words throughout the day—faithfully. I prayed for him as I washed dishes, folded laundry, shopped for groceries and made my bed. I even prayed for him before I fell asleep at night. Relinquishing that which I could not control, including any preconceived notions I may have had about relationships, I became fiercely mindful of my intentions, always focused on the abundance of love, joy and purpose in my life.

Whether I was writing Love Notes, eating dinner over the kitchen sink (alone) or evading mutiny in the middle school classroom, I kept my eye on the prize, rather than the pain. I remained grateful for all that was and all that was yet to be. I thanked God, as if it were already mine. And I believe it was that mindset, matched with God's goodness that ultimately delivered all that I asked for.

One day, early on in our mission, Mom and I were seated at a lunch counter at a restaurant that faced the headquarters of the Phoenix Police Department. We made a special trip downtown that day to distribute Love Notes. Police officers are easy pickings in the urban regions, and their patrol cars are a plenty. Firefighters, too.

While Mom nursed a cup of coffee and I wrote Love Notes, I noticed two police officers enter the sandwich shop. Mom looked at me and smiled. I grabbed a couple of LEO Love Notes from my stash and stopped the men as they got in line to order lunch. One of

the officers, a man with kind blue eyes, a sergeant named Alan, hung back and talked with me. He seemed really moved by the gesture and even agreed to take a photo. Not long after that meeting, Alan  invited me to come speak to three different police briefings at a local precinct. Each briefing was scheduled for a different shift, so I made three separate trips to the police department in one day—morning, afternoon and evening. That was cool. I got to share our love story with no less than twenty officers in each session, and I was able to deliver as many Love Notes.

I still have the callous to prove it.

Alan has since retired from the department. He has become a close friend, someone whom I respect and admire. He has also received two Love Notes from me, 1.) The LEO Love Note he got on the day we met at the sandwich shop, and 2.) A veteran Love Note I left on his car weeks later, not knowing it was him. I would also learn (much later) that Alan was connected to Chris "the street cop" Jane told me about, but more on that later.

Alan and his wife, Linda, are now writing Love Notes of their own, spreading handwritten love and gratitude to veterans and first responders as they travel across the country in their RV. I am tickled pink when Alan reaches out to tell me the stories.

Recently he called to tell me about a great airline adventure. He was flying to the Pacific Northwest, so he wrote a Love Note for the flight crew. Alan was met with a mountain of appreciation. Flight attendants gushed, offering him cookies and conversation. One of them was close to tears, which goes to show that the smallest show of kindness is a magnet for miracles—big and small.

Hey Natalie, I just want to thank you for the very thoughtful card you wrote me. I know cops aren't supposed to admit this, and I never would to my squad mates, (ha ha!) but that [nasty] note left on my car really hurt my feelings. And your note put a Band-aid on that, so thank you so much!

—Jessy A., Law Enforcement Officer

TWENTY-ONE

Friday "Knight" Lights

I n the Fall of 2018, the head of Westview High School's varsity football program, Coach Nick, called to invite me to come share our Love Note story with him, his coaching staff and their football program that included 150 male student athletes.

At the time, I had no idea if I had it in me to win over a team of teenage boys, let alone inspire so many of them to onboard the long-lost art of writing Love Notes. However, I knew I had to try. The good news: I had five things going for me: 1.) Having been a football mom, I know what makes teenage boys tick. 2.) The last time I checked, I was still middle school's "Biggest Dreamer," 3.) I had my favorite combat veteran, Jeremiah, tagging along with me to share his side of our Love Note story, 4.) The Universe is always in play, 5.) Mom didn't nickname me "Gluey" for nothing.

Remember the mama goat?

Jeremiah and I had just under two hours to convince these young men of our cause. Right away, I could see our story was resonating. Not only could you hear a pin drop in that large room, but you could also see in those boys' welled-up, watery eyes that our message was hitting home. After our presentation was complete, I am proud to say that the Westview Knights' football program became our biggest supporters, if not in squad size, in stature. Not only was the entire program onboard with getting involved that season, but they were genuinely moved by the simple gesture. That afternoon, all three teams (varsity, junior varsity and freshman) penned Love Notes addressed to our nation's heroes. I also encouraged them to write a Love Note to someone who personally inspired them—a parent, a coach, a teacher, a sibling, a friend. I wanted them to experience the "heart-melting effect" that comes with delivering a handwritten Love Note. I knew that if they felt that heightened emotion, the lesson would stick for the rest of their lives. They seemed to dig the idea!

A few weeks later, Coach Nick called to invite me to a varsity football game.

"We are honoring our first responders at our September 28th home game," he said. "And we would love it if you would be our honorary team captain."

I couldn't believe what I was hearing. Mom would have been over the moon. She was *the* biggest football fan—EVER!

"Yes," I exclaimed. "Of course!"

The very thought of attending the high school event in that capacity gave me goosebumps. It made every minute that I spent writing and delivering Love Notes worthwhile. It wasn't about the personal recognition. I wasn't in it for that. What I wanted more than anything was to be a living, breathing example of how easy it is to spread love and how quickly that love returns to its origin, restoring one's faith in humanity.

In bed that night, I wondered how Coach Nick and the Knights' football club had come into my life, and then it occurred to me. I didn't need to know the how or the why. I only needed the faith to accept it as meant to be. I also knew that I would need to make the most of my position as honorary team captain, and so the wheels started turning. And, as if on cue, the Universe began to work its magic, lining up all the right people at just the right time. The first of whom was the mother of a fallen DPS trooper. On July 25, 2018, just two months earlier, a 24-year-old Arizona trooper was killed in the line of duty. In his final days of his field training, Tyler Edenhofer was shot down in cold blood.

Elise and I attended his wake. We braced ourselves against a mean monsoon that day, as we spent no less than one hour traipsing around the church parking lot, planting over one-hundred Love Notes on patrol cars from around the country. By the time we were done, we were windblown, and we had dust and debris in our teeth, hair and eyes.

When a friend of mine got wind that I wanted to do something special at the football game, she brought up the fact that she was a fourth-grade classmate of Edenhofer's mother. This gave me an idea, not to mention an "in" to invite this woman to join me as honorary team captain. I couldn't think of a better way to honor this fallen hero and his fellow first responders then to bring her onboard. To my surprise, Trooper Edenhofer's mom, Debbie, kindly and courageously agreed. After a brief, albeit heartfelt conversation between LEO moms, I hung up the phone, and I cried. Never in my wildest dreams would I have thought I would be in a position to give back to my community in such a profound way.

Again, something bigger was at work.

There must have been because a few days after that, Jane reached out to tell me that she invited her friend, the retired street cop, to the first responder's football game.

"I invited Chris," she said. "He was one of the officers on scene when David Glasser was killed in the line of duty in 2016. He helped put down David's killer."

David Glasser.

I remembered that name ***and*** that day all too well. It happened near the time my firstborn son was swearing in as a police officer in the state of Georgia. David Glasser, the officer killed, was a young family man, not too much older than my boy. I remember how it scared me. At the time, I did the only thing I could do. I sent the effected police department a big bundle of Love Notes.

The world was shrinking.

"That's wonderful, Jane," I replied, not knowing just how wonderful, if not life changing it would be.

I had no idea how all of this was happening, but I was not about to look a gift horse in the mouth. All I knew was that none of these good people would have come into my life had Mom and I not focused on something remarkable when life took a turn for the worse. As these noteworthy names in law enforcement started showing up in my life, I suddenly felt an enormous responsibility to them and to their community. So, I took a deep breath. I stiffened my spine, and I cast my shoulders back. I had never felt stronger or more purposeful in all my life.

Somewhere in all the difficult days, I found my "thing." And, while being named "honorary team captain" was one of *the* coolest things to ever happen to me, the real gift was in the love and favor I felt from a higher source, far removed from the gridiron. It still brings tears to my eyes when I think of all the good people who were sent to me (and who stuck around) because of a Love Note.

On her deathbed, Mom said God had bigger plans for me. Maybe this is what she meant. All I know is that I was busy keeping a promise to her and to myself. I was simply watering and growing what she and I started together, a movement of love. I wasn't looking for my Knights (in shining armor). That was the last thing on my mind, but somewhere along the way, they found me.

Speaking of knights, I'll never forget when Jane's friend, the retired street cop, walked onto the sidelines that night. He showed up wearing blue jeans, a tee shirt, a ballcap and riding boots. From what I could tell, as he stood before me with a motorcycle helmet tucked under his arm, he was some kind of adventurer—on top of being a world-class warrior. And, yet, looking into his earnest brown eyes, his disposition seemed unaffected, which was kind of weird considering everything he had been through, including a twenty-year career as a police officer, burying sixteen of his brothers over the course of that career, three shootings and one god-awful gunfight that claimed the life of a fellow officer. It was Alan who gave him a ride home that night—small world! At the time, I wasn't sure what to think about it. Jane threw her arms open and gave him a great, big hug. She seemed happy to see him. I, of course, was thrilled, considering he (and Debbie) were like the paperclip I manifested a few years earlier—delivered just in the nick of time.

"Everybody ... this is Chris," Jane declared, introducing him to our little circle that included Elise, Macy, Debbie and me.

I went in for the hug. It was warm and unexpected, even with a big, awkward motorcycle helmet in play. Chris welcomed me into his arms, placing his free hand on the side of my head, gently pressing my cheek into his chest.

If I'm being honest, that hug caught me off guard. In that small moment, the cheering of the crowd hushed. The cheerleaders' chants were muffled, as was the band and the football game. I can't explain it, except to say that everything and everyone in that moment hit home. On top of which, Chris' hand on the side of my head took me back to the day Mom threw in the towel, the day she declined further treatment. I knew what that meant, so I rested my head in her lap, and I cried. I remember how her warm, bony hand felt against my head, as she softly smoothed my hair from my face.

When Jane introduced me to Chris, I had no idea that he would turn out to be such an important part of my love story. He was so unassuming. Except for that extraordinary hug and the fact that he (a storied street cop) had shown up to my event, I didn't think I'd ever see him again. There was a point in time when Debbie went MIA. Without saying a word, Chris fell back to look for her. I was touched when I learned he had taken it upon himself to follow her to the parking lot and keep her company. She was struggling. It had only been a couple of months that she buried her boy. The wound was fresh. Personally, I don't know that I would have had the courage to show up to an event like that, so soon after losing a child.

She was very brave!

Overall, the night was a huge hit. Debbie and I got to participate in the coin toss at the fifty-yard line at the start of the game. The announcer introduced us both, as well as made mention of her son Tyler Edenhofer. Both the home team *and* the visiting team wrote Love Notes honoring local first responders, which were presented during the half-time show. I received a strong show of love and support from my new circle of friends, including Coach Nick, Tonya, the Athletic Director, and the Knights varsity football team. I handed out no less than fifty Love Notes to local firefighters and law enforcement officers. And the Westview Knights took home the big "W" against Tolleson— 23 to 17. Knights in shining armor, indeed.

Natalie, this morning my son handed me one of your notes. I assume you noticed the Purple Heart on my license plate. I can't tell you how much your kindness means to me, and I'm sure, others you have touched. It's especially meaningful to me as a Vietnam Vet whose welcome home was anything but welcoming. My wife asked me how the note made me feel ... I feel little associated with the Purple Heart and resultant prosthetic leg. Those happened. What inspires me is your refreshing action—a powerful indication that folks can be simply grateful and motivated to quietly reach out and share their appreciation. Easy to say, you made my day—more importantly, you sustained an optimism often diluted day to day. Semper fidelis.

—Jim C., Purple Heart

TWENTY-TWO

Perks of a Love Note Lady

I may or may not have mentioned that there are certain perks to being the Love Note Lady. Let me first preface by saying, while the "perks" are great, that is not why I do what I do. I do what I do because it feels so good, which (technically) could be construed as a "perk," but what can I say? The feeling one gets from spreading love can oftentimes seem selfish, and that's okay. It was Pablo Picasso who said, "*The meaning of life is to find your gift. The purpose of life is to give it away.*" If what Picasso said is true, then I had, indeed, found my gift, and there are definite sweeteners to giving it away.

It had been one of those days. It was a Friday afternoon, and I was running around like a mad woman, trying to get stuff done. In my usual fashion, I had crammed one too many "to dos" on my long list of "to dos." On top of which, I had a high school football game to go to that night. The Westview Knights had made it to the state playoffs, and Coach Nick invited me to attend.

Of course, in between the game and getting stuff done, two of my favorite Love Note ambassadors, Sherri and her ten-year-old son, Wyatt, reached out to tell me that they had a big bundle of Love Notes to give me. They were literally just down the road in the parking lot outside of Sam's Club. I was in the vicinity, so I figured I would pop over and pick up the bundle with time to spare. No problem.

Right?

Well, when I pulled into the parking lot, I was so happy to see my friends, that I jumped out of my Jeep, shut the door behind me and ran over to greet them with great, big bear hugs. Sherri was pushing a grocery cart stuffed to the gills with food, mostly meat and fresh goods. As I went to tuck the bundle of Love Notes in my Jeep, I quickly realized I had locked the keys inside.

Dang it! I knew I should have invested in AAA.

Embarrassed, I turned to Sherri and Wyatt and said, "Uh oh."

Wyatt, my all-time favorite ambassador, went into hero mode and exclaimed, "Mom, we can't just leave her here!"

"No," I begged. "You two go home. You have all this food and meat. I don't want any of it to go bad. I will figure this out on my own."

"We are *not* leaving you," Wyatt exclaimed.

Sherri agreed.

"I am going back into the store to talk to the manager.

Maybe he has a Slim Jim or something," Wyatt said, taking off in the direction of Sam's Club.

I apologized up and down to Sherri. She, of course, smiled graciously and shrugged it off, which made me feel even worse. When Wyatt returned without a Slim Jim, Sherri called her boyfriend Brian for backup. Meanwhile, the frost on the packages of meat was melting, and it was getting dark. On top of which, the Knights had surely kicked off their first playoff game.

We waited for Brian to arrive on scene, and when he did, we huddled around him as he attempted to finagle the door lock with a metal gadget a passerby had given us from the back of his truck. It was soon clear that there was no way we were getting into my Jeep, not without an expensive locksmith or a genie in a bottle. That's when I made a last-ditch phone call to Scott, a firefighter friend and Love Note recipient. I asked him if, by chance, firefighters offered a complimentary service to local yocals who lock their keys in the car.

"Is there a baby inside the car?" he asked, chuckling.

"Nope," I shrugged. "Just my humility."

"I'll see what I can do."

The next thing I knew, Peoria Fire Engine 193 came barreling into the parking lot—no lights, no siren. I waved them down, and within five minutes, I had my car keys in my hand and a photograph with Wyatt and the firefighters to capture the moment. Wyatt handed out Love Notes to the pack of heroes who had just sat down to dinner when they got the call. I was so embarrassed!

Mostly, I was grateful. It was proof that the good you put into the world returns to you. If *that* brand of love and kindness isn't a perk of being a Love Note Lady, then I don't know what is.

When we first began this mission, Mom insisted that we weren't to ask anything of any one of our Love Note recipients, lest it lessen the act of kindness. At the time, I agreed with her. However, I came to understand that when you give to others in good faith, you have to be equally open to receive goodness in return. The fact is people want to be good to those who are good to them. Kindness mirrors itself. It is love's ripple effect. Giving back is the very nature of kindness, and it is what intrinsically connects us as humans.

I am so grateful for Sherri, Wyatt and Brian. Not just because they stayed behind until the calvary came, but because they continue to "push the envelope" in their community. They continue to push Mom's legacy of love, and I see it in Sherri's teary eyes every time we meet how much it means to them.

Thank you, Sherri and Wyatt!

As luck would have it, (Or should I say love?), I made it to the Knights' playoff game. I got there at the end of half time, just as the team was taking the field. Coach Nick and I locked eyes, and the next thing I knew he locked his arm around my neck and pulled me onto the sidelines with the team. It felt like some kind of miracle. Partly because I made it to the game at all, and partly because it was the same football field my boys had practiced and played on a few years before. Mom and I had spent countless hours watching and cheering on my boys from those very bleachers at Liberty High

School. At one point, I looked up into the home stands and smiled. I could almost feel her in the crowd of faces. She would have loved this, for all the same reasons I did, which is what made missing her hurt so badly.

The Knights lost the game that night, which compounded the feeling of loss. And, of course, there were tears, as the team huddled up together in the end zone for one last heart-to-heart with their coaches. Their heads hung low, but their spirits were strong. For some, it would be their last football game—ever. When they were done, the quarterback walked over to me and thanked me.

"You changed my life," he said. "I won't ever forget you."

"Thank you," I smiled.

And to think, I didn't know if I had it in me to reach these young men with a simple handwritten Love Note. As I walked off the field that night, car keys in hand, surrounded by a group of young men who fought the good fight, I felt a part of something special. And I realized, even in defeat, marred with blood, sweat and tears, these boys showed up and gave their all. Which goes to show, if something matters enough, it becomes our duty to give our best effort, even if the odds aren't in our favor.

Sending love to so many "someones" is <u>so</u> awesome. I hope you take a moment today to sit back and absorb what you and your mom started. Thank you for letting me be a small part of your mission. The world is a better place because of you!

—Candie D.

TWENTY-THREE
Badge Bunny

Mom could always be counted on to play devil's advocate. For instance, she would often caution me to the fact that police wives might not appreciate some random woman handing their hubbies Love Notes while they were on duty. To be fair, I could see her point. I mean, it wasn't like I hadn't thought about it. In fact, one Arizona trooper chuckled when I handed him a Love Note outside of a Chick-Fil-A—his second.

"I got one of your notes on my patrol vehicle awhile back," the trooper smiled. "When my wife read it, she was *very* curious to know who Natalie was and why she was writing me a Love Note."

I giggled, somewhat embarrassed. Being a woman, myself, I understood that it was a reasonable reaction for a wife to have, and probably not the first in the history of this mission. However, I didn't let it stop me. This pursuit was so much more than a cheeky flirtation, and I knew that people would realize it soon enough.

That's not to say that there hasn't been the opportunity to flirt a little. I mean, the last time I checked, I still had a pulse, and I often find myself surrounded by attractive men and women in uniform—firefighters, police officers and military servicemen. However, because this mission means so much to me, and because it is making such a positive impact on the community at large, I never wanted to taint that with shallow inuendo. I suppose that's why I do my level best to keep it professional.

The truth of the matter is police wives, by and large, have been some of my biggest supporters. That's not to say that I haven't been accused of being a "badge bunny" once or twice when a police wife posts pictures of a Love Note online, asking the sixty-four-thousand-dollar question, "Who is this badge bunny, and why is she writing *my* husband a Love Note?"

It's all very Elmer Fudd.

Be vewy, vewy quiet. It's wabbit season. ☺

The good news is, when that happens, the majority of law enforcement wives stand up and vouch for me and my Love Notes. I was told by one LEO wife, another Natalie, a soul sister of sorts, that she responds to those quips with, "Nah, that's just the *other* Natalie. We love her!"

Nothing (but love) to see here, ladies!

This is why I work so hard to keep this endeavor true blue, particularly with law enforcement. They are a community to whom one must earn their trust, and it's no wonder why when you consider what these heroes are up against from one call to the next.

I, for one, never want my effort to dishearten those on the receiving end of this gesture, least of all a population of police wives because more often than not, they are *the* heart and soul behind the badge. I just love them all to death—one in particular. Her name is Danielle. On the outside, she is picture perfect, a real heartbreaker. On top of which, she is fit as a fiddle. You almost want to hate her. She is that beautiful, but it's her big heart that wins you over, time and time again. Her heart was the first thing I saw and felt when she walked through the door that first day we met. Before I could even introduce myself, she grabbed hold of me and hugged me, like there was no tomorrow.

Seriously! It's a good thing I wasn't a jelly donut.

It was coming up on the one-year anniversary of Mom's death. I didn't know it, but I was forming my tribe. After seeing several posts about Love Notes on the Arizona Law Enforcement Wives Network Facebook page, she took a chance and reached out to me. She wrote: "*Hi Natalie, I first wanted to let you know that I'm truly inspired by your love notes. My husband is a former Marine and is currently a K9 handler. I frequently see your open posts to join you to write love notes. However, it's usually not at a time I can manage, as we have four kids, and timing is everything. I am looking to do some different volunteering with my girls (ages 11 and 10). I would love to find a time to sit down and write love notes with you and them. Being a part of the Blue family, you and your notes are famous! After the first couple of notes I saw posted, I decided to look you up. I have been following you now for probably a year. Thanks, Danielle*"

Of course, always happy to recruit new writers, I invited her to meet up at a Starbuck's somewhere in between her house and mine. I am always eager to get outside of my routine and meet new people, especially after losing Mom, my partner in crime. My boys were already out of the nest with lives of their own, and so it was good for the soul to befriend new faces. I didn't realize how good it could be until I met this particular woman and her family.

As soon as I met her, I was blown away by her breadth and beauty. And her daughters were just as lovely. The thing that made them especially beautiful was their makeup—not the kind you'd find behind a cosmetics counter, but the inner makings of their disposition and character. In that way, all three girls were dazzling. On top of which, they were sweet, warm and wonderful. And they seemed pretty smitten with my mission.

Danielle's girls, Chloe and Andie, made a fierce first impression, writing handfuls of Love Notes for two hours straight, while Danielle and I got to know one another. To look at us, you would have thought we were long, lost friends, catching up after years of separation. I think that is (overwhelmingly!) one of the biggest takeaways from this endeavor—the magnetism of goodness and the immediate connection I feel with perfect strangers.

Danielle is just one of those people who loves and cares fiercely. You feel it in every hug and in every good deed she does. I think sometimes she worries that it's not enough, but when I look at her four beautiful children, her lovely home, her knack for work/life balance in an executive role and in the vast ocean that is her heart, I am reminded of one of my favorite Mother Teresa quotes that reads, *"If you want to change the world, go home and love your family."*

That is Danielle all day long.

I am blessed to have her in my life and in my corner, not just because she puts me up every time I come into town or gives me a platform to tell our story at her workplace or keeps me in card stock and stitches, but because she is proof (once again) that when you are doing the right things, the right things happen, like attracting good people into your circle. These beautiful women behind the badge are the real deal. They love fiercely, and Danielle is just the tip of the iceberg. There is Mylinda, Natalie, Andrea, Kelsea, Lexie, Sarah, Alex, and Kary—to name a few. I just love them all!

They helped me prove Mom wrong, and that's not an easy thing to do. It turns out these wonderful women who love the sound of Velcro, also love knowing not everybody hates their husbands. Not only do they get behind Love Notes being given to their husbands, but they get behind me, the woman handing them out because they get how much these notes are needed, now more than ever! One police wife, Mylinda, said it best, *"I can't tell you how much it encourages us as spouses when we see the community appreciating our officers. It gives us strength to continue sending them out into the dark world day after day. It's very brave of you to show your support out loud when the mob might be louder. And it really strengthens those of us who, in the moment, feel very weak."*

One of our deputies received a card on his patrol unit while staying at the San Bernardino Hilton during the Dominic Vaca services. He shared the note with our Honor Guard team. I just want to reach out and tell you thank you! I appreciate all you do! Thank you, thank you, thank you!

—Karyse S., Law Enforcement Officer

TWENTY-FOUR

My Favorite Things

O ne of the unexpected (and most valuable) verticals in our Love Note mission has been to inspire today's youth to not only recognize and appreciate those who courageously protect the front lines of our country and communities, but to express an outward show of gratitude toward them.

I spent a couple of years working as a substitute teacher, and one of my greatest revelations, aside from how underappreciated schoolteachers are these days, is that most students don't know how to write their way out of a paper bag, not a letter, not a research paper, not a resume—nada. That's why I always made it a point to share my story. I believe there are a handful of lessons here:

1. **Respect for Authority**: To be grateful for one's freedom is to be grateful for and respect those who stand/stood to defend it. A respectful country is a stronger country.

2. **Honoring Tradition**: Handwriting letters is a dying art, and if lost, we lose a critical element in genuine communication, that "X-factor" that moves humans, connects them more profoundly than any piece of digital technology ever will.

3. **Giving Thanks**: Gratitude changes EVERYTHING!

Inspiring our nation's youth to handwrite Love Notes to those who inspire them is one of my favorite parts of this mission. Whether students write a letter to their mom, dad, brother, sister, teacher, coach, first responder, veteran, military serviceman and/or

the President of the United States, they are creating timeless connections. There is, indeed, power in the pen. There is also strength in numbers. I had my niece and nephew, Alexis and Chase, writing and delivering Love Notes, as well as a young girl named Presley who created original artwork on her Love Notes. She also inspired her peers to get involved as a project for school.

As someone who spent the better part of her time writing Love Notes alone at a coffee shop, I am most grateful for all the help I can get in championing this movement and in building Love Note bundles for our nation's heroes across the country. As many as I have personally written over the past (almost) six years, there is just no way to keep up with the demand. This part of my love story is where God opened up a window and a breath of fresh air blew in, multiplying the amount of love we were able to distribute.

That breath of fresh air's name is Colleen.

When Colleen first reached out to me, she was a high school English teacher. She invited me, Jeremiah, Zach and Danielle into her classroom to speak to her students. The four of us shared our individual Love Note stories, hoping to inspire students with Love Notes of their own. From that day forward, Colleen has bolstered this mission with thousands and thousands of Love Notes for veterans and first responders—from two separate high schools. It literally takes my breath away, not to mention an entire year to distribute them all.

No matter what is happening in Colleen's life, she is always there, looking for ways to spread love in her community. As I mentioned, that's when the magic happens, when you are doing something good in the world ... when you least feel like it. Colleen has been a notable part of this love story. She was one of the first to believe in me and my mission, periodically bringing me in to speak with students, surprising me with news coverage and a generous gift card to keep me in supply of card stock **and** creating an entire night for first responders at a varsity football game. That was all in an effort to encourage her kids to give back to a community she loves.

I'll always love her for that.

It's that unaffected sense of faith, fortitude and affection that helps us to survive our darkest days. It's not always easy to see the silver lining in life, and sometimes the last thing you want to do is be nice when life (and the people in it) are anything but. However, I can tell you with complete confidence that something as simple as writing a Love Note, even on days when life has got you licked, can turn adversity on its ear. And my mission's success is due, in part, to educators like Colleen and Coach Nick who care about their students, their community and the future. Rebecca, the wife of one of my favorite firefighters and Love Note recipients, is also a highly-respected, high-school teacher. She invited Jeremiah and me to speak to her students, and so they too are a noteworthy part of this love story. There are days I have to pinch myself. And then there are days when I know it has all been a part of God's divine plan. Seeing as how it saved me, how could it not be?

Another of my favorite parts of the Love Note mission is giving people pause—a time out, of sorts. If you ask me, we are all way too busy these days. So, when the opportunity presents itself, a chance to stop someone in their tracks, I take it. Nothing

pleases me more than to catch someone plucking a Love Note from their windshield and taking time to read it. I swear, it never gets old.

Love Notes are the pause button—personified.

One day I was visiting with a girlfriend at a local coffee

shop. I was gazing out of the big, pane-glass window, as a woman pulled into the parking lot. She had a Gold Star Family license plate, signifying the loss of a loved one while serving in the armed forces. I caught my breath. I was carrying a Gold Star Family Love Note.

"Hold that thought," I whispered, cutting my friend off mid-sentence. I quickly rifled through my purse, thumbing through a thick stack of Love Notes written for veterans, law enforcement officers, firefighters, military servicemen and (ah ha!) ... GOLD STAR FAMILY!

Yes!

The woman pushed through the coffee shop door. As she stepped up to the counter to pick up her mobile order, I snuck outside, into the parking lot and planted the Love Note on the driver side window. I narrowly escaped getting caught in the act. I literally brushed shoulders with the woman on my way back into the café. My girlfriend and I watched intently as the woman returned to her car with a steaming, hot cup of coffee in hand. She froze, as she reached for the door handle. Studying the white envelope tucked into the window sleeve, she looked to her left and then to her right. The steam from her coffee swirled upward in a January gust. Gently lifting the Love Note with long, slender fingers, she got into her car and shut the door behind her. The woman started the engine and sat in that parking spot for no less than fifteen minutes. I can only imagine what was going through her mind. All I know is that in the craziness of our day, pause is a really good thing, especially with a warm cup of Joe (and a Love Note) in hand to console us.

You are the best! I've been the recipient of your generosity, and it made me feel amazing! I actually teared up as I read it! Keep doing your thing! It really means a lot and makes a difference! I still have mine; I see it every day because it's displayed behind my desk.

—Dean C., Veteran

TWENTY-FIVE

Plot Twist

Sixteen months after losing Mom, my life was in flux. I was working two parttime jobs—accounts receivable for a local, family-owned tire company in the morning and substitute teaching for a local school district in the afternoon.

It was all I could do to make ends meet.

For a grounded girl, someone who had colored inside the lines at a Fortune 100 company for twenty years and who, at one point, landed the "corner office" at a major university, the piecemeal paycheck was, well, uncomfortable, to say the least—no health benefits, no 401K, no vacation time, no nada. And yet, in some weird way, I found the upset to my routine and work life kind of exotic. It was so far removed from life as I knew it. It allowed me to experiment. I mean, if we never dare to color outside the lines, how else do we make for a great life story, not to mention break routine?

Right?

I had spent the better part of two years caring for Mom, getting her to doctor appointments, tracking her medications, cleaning up medical waste and so forth. Before that, it was twenty years of bringing up boys while working a job that never quite fit.

Routine was my middle name.

This was the first time in my adult life I wasn't holding down a soul-crushing, corporate-cubicle career, whilst carpooling kids to and from school and football practice, packing sack lunches, and throwing together last-minute science projects. I wasn't having to get creative in the kitchen, so as to feed a small army of neighborhood kids and make decisions based on everyone else's needs and schedules. I had gone rogue. I had escaped the institution, so to speak. I was Terminator II's Sarah Connor, only not as buffed and badass.

Don't get me wrong. I loved being a mother and a daughter. I would do it all over again, but the next chapter in my story was all up to me. There were no excuses to be had, or people to point fingers at. It was all on me, and while it was scary as hell, there was a growing sense of anticipation. It literally gave me butterflies.

I did my best to embrace the unknown. It wasn't like I hadn't been there before. I had gotten good at starting over, writing new chapters in my life. Although, up until now, most of those "new chapters" were based on my life's decisions. Therefore, the composition of each chapter had already been outlined for me.

My 20s were all about being married with children. My 30s were all about finding my feet as an independent woman and a single mom, doing my best not to wreck my boys' childhood following divorce. My 40s sent me back to school to finally finish up my four-year degree and to circumnavigate the Sandwich Generation, a unique doorway in time that appeared in the middle of bringing up boys and caring for my dying mother.

Talk about a rock and a hard place.

And now, as I embark upon my 50s, God only knows what is next, but so as not to leave too much to chance, I stay focused on the positive and the things I want most from my life. This is my fresh slate—a reboot for my future. And I intend to make the most of it.

I am finding that with each decade I am stronger than the last. I am more myself, and even though it can be hard sometimes, it is the uncharted, rocky roads that lead to the most meaningful destinations. I suppose that's why I allowed myself to float around for a little while after Mom died. I spent time growing Love Notes, making new friends, role playing with my local police departments, partaking in a number of police ride alongs, taking long naps, and simply breathing. Oh, and I got a tattoo!

That was sort of a big deal.

Because I had no one to answer to, I got to do the things I loved, which meant not having to feel guilty for taking time away from my family. And while I desperately missed Mom and my boys, it was kind of nice not having to think about everyone else's needs first, not having to cook forty pounds of pasta after football practice, but rather eating alone, standing over the kitchen sink, cats circling my feet, foraging for drippings from my pre-cooked chicken roaster, a single girl's best friend.

I slept in the buff. I took baths in the middle of the day. I went to movies late at night. I reveled in my own company. It was great! There was no one to tell me that I was a "mean mom" for making them take out the garbage or clean up the yard waste, or that I needed to move up a deadline, or that I should take the scrunchie out of my hair. It was just me, and while it could be lonely at times, especially at night, it was all kinds of cathartic. After a while, I could hear that still, small voice inside of me again, and that voice was sounding brave and raring to go, wherever the wind might take her.

The Universe must have gotten wind because at the start of 2019, I received three pivotal phone calls that would lay the groundwork for the "next big chapter," expanding my options exponentially. All three phone calls were (unsolicited) writing gigs, two of which were referred to me by Bob Duffy.

The first phone call came from a professional soccer player, a friend of Bob's, who I will call Donnie. His story is one of true daring—the stuff of David and Goliath. Helping him write his story affected me profoundly. It forced me out of my shell and proved my high school guidance counselor wrong when he said that I would never be able to make a living as a writer.

Yeah right!

The second call was, as I mentioned earlier, from a Silicon

Valley phenom named Carol Latham. She was looking for an editor for her book. She had written her life story and what a story! When she was my age, she created a material designed to cool digital devices, like computers, laptops, air-conditioning units and the cell phone attached to your hip. She's amazing, and the courage it took her to take her invention to market (in a man's world) is unmatched. I couldn't believe she found me, and that she would ask for *my* help.

These successful, self-made individuals could have hired anyone to tell their story, but they hired me. Truth be told, I wouldn't be here now without them and the work they paid me well for. I was finally able to quit my two parttime gigs and breathe a little easier.

The third, and probably the most life-changing phone call, came from Jane's friend, Chris, the retired street cop. His book, a true tale of survival on the mean streets of Maryvale in Phoenix, Arizona, needed an editor, and even though I had two other writing gigs in the works, I was eager to take his onboard. I was confident that I had it in me to do all three. Honestly, I would have been a fool to pass on any one of them.

How could I?

Seriously.

Each was a divine gift, the kind you don't return. I was grateful for all three opportunities, and even though on some level I was spreading myself thin, I knew there had to be a reason why they showed up when they did. It was a lot of responsibility, but I knew I could do it. I think the Universe knew it too, which is why I believe I crossed paths with the retired street cop again.

I was headed to the Executive Terminal at Sky Harbor Airport for a police training event. It was a little after 7:00 a.m. I was running late, due in part to rush hour traffic and a minor fender bender on the freeway. It was just a small tap on my back bumper, no damage to either one of us—not even a scratch. The young man, a teenager, who hit me was devastated, near tears.

"I'm so sorry," he cried. "I didn't mean to hit you."

"It's fine," I said, giving him a hug. "No harm. No foul."

The poor guy was trembling as he returned to his dad's car.

"Nothing to see here," I sighed, feeling pressed for time.

I quickly texted Elise before I jumped back in the car and jockeyed for position. I had to let her know I was running late. Traffic was suddenly at a crawl.

Damn rubberneckers.

As I ambled into the large conference room, the early morning briefing was just about to wrap up. I took the last seat at the far end of the room, opposite Elise. It was another scenario-based training day, an all-day affair that would focus on airport surveillance. The room was stocked full of law enforcement personnel, active and retired, and as many civilian volunteers, me and Elise included. We had been recruited as role players for a full day of training with the next class of officers.

There were two scenarios. Because I showed up late, the training officer in charge assigned me to the second scenario, the one opposite Elise. She and I looked at each other from across the room, sighing in disappointment. We had never been separated before. In our minds, we were a package deal. It was always the two of us in the first scenario—except for that day.

The meeting adjourned, and the room slowly stood to its feet and shuffled toward the shuttle bus out front. We were being herded to the airport terminal to assume our positions. I was bummed. Elise and I always made the most of training days, and being that it was an all-day affair, I couldn't imagine roleplaying without her, but everything happens for a reason.

Right?

It suddenly dawned on me that my friend Jane and Chris, the retired street cop, were in my scenario. I hadn't seen either one of them since the night of the football game, nor had I seen Chris at one of these training events.

"Hey you! It's good to see you," I smiled.

"Same, same," he replied, pulling me into a hug.

Chris and Jane had been paired up to pose as a couple. I was cast as a lone traveler. It was our job to blend in and, at some point, execute a bag exchange. I was supposed to drop a bag somewhere in the airport for Chris and Jane to pick up. It was all very James Bond—Skyfall at Sky Harbor. The whole point was to train officers to surveil in these types of "sneaky" scenarios, catch us in the act, so to speak.

After each scenario, we would meet up with the evaluators and the officers in training and debrief. As soon as we were done, we would reset the scenario and begin again for the next group. This went on all day. In between scenarios, Chris and I got to talking. He told me about his book and asked if he could send it to me via email.

"Jane says you're an editor," he said. "Would you mind taking a look at my book?"

"Of course," I smiled. "Be happy to."

Chris emailed me his manuscript. I heard the notification ping my phone. I was starting to feel like Clarence in "It's a Wonderful Life"— *"Every time a bell rings, an angel gets his wings."* Only instead of a bell it was an email notification and instead of wings, it was an amazing book project. I looked up toward Heaven and shook my head. Within one month, I had three inspiring stories in my safekeeping—three big book projects. Mom might have had something to do with that. I certainly hadn't solicited for the work.

At lunch, I reconnected with Elise. We sat down for a little over an hour at a long table in the middle of the terminal and broke bread with our fellow volunteers—people who, if I had tried to connect with, I could not have—not in a million years.

In between bites, I opened Chris' email. There it was. The manuscript—the game changer. I began reading it. I was instantly hooked. I couldn't peel my eyes away. I lost all sense of time and space. Immediately, I knew that of all stories that had been placed in my safekeeping, the one that was going to change my life, at least professionally, was his. I felt it in my bones.

After lunch, just before training was about to resume, I

approached the lead trainer to see if I could switch to scenario number one to be with Elise.

Denied.

"Dude," he exclaimed. "Stick it out. We're almost done."

It must have been meant to be because just as we were about to set up another scenario, Chris touched me on the sleeve and said, "Let's switch things up. How about you and I partner up?"

I looked up at him and smiled.

"Are you good with that," he asked.

"Sure," I shrugged, "Fine by me."

I glanced over at Jane. She seemed less than thrilled about the change up. Chris edged up next to me, his hand finding the small of my back. We ambled through the airport terminal together, a make-believe couple in a police-training scenario. It was our first chance at a real conversation. We talked about his book, the possibilities and the work it would take to get it published. We became so engrossed, there were times we forgot about the training that was taking place and missed our cue for the big "bag exchange." Chris even forgot his laptop bag on a nearby bench, which could have been catastrophic, considering his book-to-be was onboard.

Chris was so easy to be around. For a street cop with so much bad stuff under his belt, his warm disposition was disarming. As a book editor, I was sensing a paradigm shift happening, a fundamental change leading up to something new (and exciting) in my own story. It was a pleasant plot twist sporting a pair of old cowboy boots and a book deal.

I received one of your notes, and I had to reach out to say it not only made my day, but it made my week! I have shown it to my friends and coworkers, and I still get emotional. I know you did this and expect nothing in return, but I want you to know how much this means to me. I plan on putting it in a frame and hanging it in my office, so I can share our story. Every time I look at the note, it will put a smile on my face. Thank you.

—Todd S., U.S. Military Veteran

TWENTY-SIX
Book Editor Lady

C hris and I met the following week to discuss his book project. What was meant to be a short meeting over lunch, turned into a five-hour conversation in a booth at a Chili's restaurant. We literally outlived two wait-staff shifts, and we were edging into happy hour. We discussed his publishing options, and he opened up to me about how the book came to be and how his law enforcement career had led him to retire after twenty years and sixty-four days.

Following his retirement, Chris was invited into the public speaking arena to share his story of survival with law enforcement agencies across the country. His passion for helping other officers only deepened my original opinion, which was that he needed to publish this work. I had all the faith in the world that his was an important story to tell, a much-needed read for law enforcement officers—past, present and future. And I was beginning to believe that it would probably be *the* most important book project of my life.

Five hours later, we reached an agreement. I would be his book editor, and in exchange for my services, I would take a percentage of the book (and film) profits. On top of which, when the book was completed, he was to throw in the Portsmouth sweatshirt he had on his person. That was *my* stipulation to the contract. We solidified the agreement with a handshake and, of course, a hug.

I think the thing that initially attracted me to Chris and his story was how earnest he was about putting something out into the world that would help others. The more time I spent with him, in person and within the pages of his manuscript, the more I felt an obligation to get his story out there. It weighed heavily on me.

There were days and nights when I was in the thick of editing that I would crawl into a hot bath at the end of the day and just cry. Some of the stories were so intense. Some were heartwarming. And some made me laugh out loud. As a mother to a law enforcement officer, there are some things I just don't want to know about the job, things I can never unknow thanks to this book. Still, it was a good read for someone who had no idea the dangers and the damage that comes with a career in law enforcement.

The more I read, the more I appreciated Chris, not just for what he did to keep our streets safe, but for having the wherewithal to come out of such a long and storied career in one solid piece. He seemed relatively healthy—mentally, physically and emotionally. It wasn't without a lot of help and counseling, and it didn't come without a toll. It cost Chris his marriage, a career that he loved, friendships and even certain connections with family. I think that's the loss that hurts him most, the cutting of family ties, especially since he has so few.

Over time, I found myself developing feelings for this man. I fought them, of course, because 1.) He was a client, 2.) I wasn't convinced he and Jane weren't a thing, and 3.) The guy had terrible eating habits. I mean, how many candy bars can one man consume in a day? All kidding aside, Chris started texting, asking to buy me breakfast or dinner. He'd invite me to go hiking. We'd often meet up and after discussing the book for no more than twenty minutes, we'd jump straight into more personal topics.

There was definitely something brewing.

And, yet it wasn't blatantly obvious at first. The man had me listed in his cell phone contacts as "Book Girl Natalie." In fact, when his friends would call while we were out hiking or having lunch, he would say, "I'll call you back later. I'm hiking with my book editor lady."

I had been reduced to his "book editor lady."

That would ultimately be the slap upside the head, the not-so-gentle reminder that this was a business deal—plain and simple. That's not to say I was disappointed—necessarily. I wasn't expecting him to refer to me as his "lady friend" or something more personal—"Natalie" would have been nice.

The one thing I did (and still do) appreciate about Chris is that he is the consummate gentleman, never taking advantage of a good thing. He's the man who opens car doors, walks on the outside of the sidewalk, pulls out your chair for you, keeps you safe in dark alleys and is perversely respectful. Seriously, bathroom humor is lost on this man. His tact is intact, which is uncommon these days. I've never seen him spit or heard him curse around the ladies. He prides himself on being a gentleman, and I, for one, love that about him. His cowboy boots and flannel shirts are just gravy!

One day I needed a ride to the airport. I was picking up a rental car for a trip to California to babysit a friend's beach condo, and because I was beginning to get the sense that Chris was one of those guys, the kind you can count on, I mustered the courage to ask him for a ride. It wasn't easy for me. I am independent to a fault, and it wasn't like I couldn't have asked my youngest son to take me. However, I am not so sure I could have counted on him showing up at five o'clock in the morning to pick me up.

Let's just say I was putting myself out there.

That morning I was dressed and ready to go an hour before Chris was scheduled to pick me up. It was still dark outside, and I was a nervous wreck. As I paced between the kitchen and my bedroom, I could hear Mom's voice, "*You are shameless.*"

As usual, she would have been right. When I heard his super-sized Super Duty pull in front of my house, my heart leapt.

Breathe, Book Editor Lady! Breathe.

It was ridiculous, really. I don't know why I was so nervous, except to say that I was beginning to like Chris—a lot. When the doorbell rang, I grabbed hold of the doorknob, took a deep breath and exhaled all the nerves and subsequent butterflies. I waited for them to flit away before I opened the door.

"Good morning," I said, as I stepped onto the front stoop.

"Morning," he replied, widening his enormous arm span for another of his great, big bear hugs.

He was not making this easy for me, as I pretended not to feel anything more than grateful for the ride. On the drive to the airport, Chris looked over at me and smiled. The sun was taking its sweet time coming up over the mountains.

"Do you think you might have time for one stop?" he asked.

"What do you have in mind?"

"Well, I thought I'd take you to the scene," he replied. "It's on the way to the airport, and it might give you some perspective in editing the book."

Just breathe.

"Sure," I said, barely breaking a whisper.

"Yeah?"

"Yeah," I agreed.

I was still battling butterflies, and so I took a deep breath. I couldn't help but wonder how I ended up in this man's truck, editing his book and headed to a scene that I had only read about in the headlines. Mind you, I had never solicited my work as a book editor, and yet there I was, poised perfectly within the pages of yet another really important story. I came upon this career (and this man) quite innocently, and it was then that I began to wonder if Chris was *the* man I had been praying for. In my prayer, I asked God to keep safe the "good man" who would love me, so that he could find his way to me. And the way this man was beginning to look at me, it was starting to feel like it could be him.

As we drove into the suburban, cookie-cutter neighborhood, the very place Chris' last gunfight took place, I began to feel a tad nauseous. He parked his truck along the sidewalk, and we found our way to the spot where all hell broke loose. The morning light was still a little murky, as he walked me through the horror of that awful day. He pointed out his scouting position, where the other officers landed as they rolled up on scene and where the twenty-year-old man—high on drugs and armed with his dad's 9mm—was lying in wait.

We stood where Chris stood that day when shots rang out. The suspect got off six shots from inside a van, three at David Glasser and three at Chris. David caught two. Chris caught zero. Eventually, we landed in the sacred spot where David Glasser was mortally wounded. I stared down at that notable piece of pavement, picturing a mother's worst nightmare come to life, tears burning at the backs of my eyes. Chris got quiet. I could see he was dealing with his emotions from that day.

"Thank you for bringing me here. It can't be easy for you."

"Thank you for letting me share it with you."

This was a big deal, not just for the book, but for the "book editor lady." I could feel Chris slowly peeling back the layers, inviting me into his life, beginning with the hardest parts. For guys like him, cynical-cop types, active and retired, that's saying something.

As he opened the truck door for me, our eyes met. We smiled, and it was on that cool morning that I felt a wave of warmth run through me. I hadn't felt that in a very long time. It suddenly occurred to me that the gunfight that materialized on that street in south Phoenix and Chris' subsequent battle to survive it was taking place at the same time as Mom's battle with cancer, at a time when I was praying my hardest and not just for her. I was praying for the good man who was bound to come into my life.

Was this the "good man?"

In my prayer, I asked God to deliver him "safely" to me, so that he might show up for me with all his heart. I looked around that scene one last time, trying to wrap my head around all that had transpired there, and I wondered if God had, indeed, answered my prayer that day—May 18, 2016. I looked at Chris as he threw the truck into drive, and we rumbled toward the airport together, both of us in one piece. Just in case it was true, I cast a silent prayer up into the heavens. Nothing but the words, *"Thank you!"*

In acknowledgement of the acts of kindness you have displayed to our country's veterans, law enforcement, firefighters, the families of the fallen officers/firefighters, etc. Your dedicated passion of "spreading the love, one note at a time" is a labor of love and true compassion to people who are surely touched by your well wishes.

—Doug Ducey., Governor of Arizona

TWENTY-SEVEN
Windsor Knot

I
f you were to ask me what tipped the scale in favor of Chris and me becoming a thing, I would tell you it had to do with a Windsor knot. Chris, on the other hand, would tell you it had to do with me taking my shoes off and planting my feet up on the dashboard somewhere just outside of Dateland while on a road trip to San Diego.

"That's when I knew I had you," he boasts.

For the record, he did not "have" me.

What he *did* have was a job interview for an instructorship at the Miramar Marine Base in San Diego. We were only a handful of weeks into a working relationship when he invited me to drive out to California  with him—one hotel room, two double beds.

"So, what do you think," he asked. "Do you feel like driving out to San Diego with me?"

Mind you, I was literally in California, babysitting my friend's beach condo when he asked.

"Can I ask you a question before I give you an answer?"

"Go," he said.

"Okay … and this is important. Are you and Jane a thing? Because she's a friend."

"I'm well aware," Chris replied. "She and I are close, but not romantically."

"Pinkie swear?"

"Scouts honor. I don't want to ruin anything between her and I. I don't want to ruin anything between you and her. And I certainly don't want to jeopardize OUR future either."

Our future? Oh man! I was in trouble.

The truth is, I still wasn't sure about Chris—romantically speaking. I mean, 1.) He was still a client, and 2.) The man packed a box fan for the road trip. I found it in the backseat of his Super Duty, both of which were dust ridden and a little worse for the wear.

"What is this contraption?" I asked.

"It's my fan. I can't sleep without it," he smiled. "Why?"

Damn those dimples.

"It comes off a little Sanford and Son, like something you'd find at your local junk dealer."

"I need it to drown out the noise."

Chris shot me a sideways look, as if he were referring to the "noise" coming from my mouth. I appreciated his sense of humor, and the fact that he didn't take himself (or my commentary) too serious. That's a good trait in a man, as is tolerance. However, it was the traveling box fan that had me stumped. If that wasn't a redneck flag, I'm not sure what was.

Truth: I was constantly trying to talk myself out of this man. If it wasn't the box fan, it was that he ate too much junk food, or that he wore nothing but blue line t-shirts and blue jeans, or that he was more than five-years separated, but not "officially" divorced. All that said, the more I tried to deny the impulse to let down my guard around him, the tougher it got.

It was freezing cold the morning of Chris' job interview. The dank hotel room was pitch dark, except for a thin slice of light that broke through the curtains. I was wide awake, wondering what Mom would think of me taking a road trip with a perfect stranger. As if the dumpster meetup wasn't bad enough, but now this?! For the record, I did share my whereabouts with Danielle and my brother, lest I go missing and no one know when (and with whom) I was last seen.

I watched as Chris quietly rolled out of bed. He skulked around in the dark (in his boxer briefs!), so as not to wake me. I pretended to be asleep, as he gathered up the chunky, knit blanket from his bed and softly laid it over top of me. I couldn't tell if he was patently smitten with me or if he was just a really great guy. To be perfectly honest, it could have been a bit of both. I mean, there was a moment the night before when I complained of back pain from the long drive, and he offered to give me a back rub. There was a moment, after I accepted, that I thought my virtue was at stake, but the man did not take advantage. He was a gentleman—all the way.

It was me who almost jumped his bones.

If you spend any time with Chris, you know that he is a protector, in every sense of the word. He may have retired from law enforcement, but he has never taken off the proverbial uniform. It is his second skin. He is ever-vigilant, especially when it comes to a lady. He is an old-fashioned, walk-on-the-outside-of-the-sidewalk, open-your-door kind of man. I think it's one of the things I like most about him. As an old-fashioned girl who has spent most of her life taking care of herself (and others), it felt good to be taken care of. Plainly, one of the things that Chris likes about me is that I let him. He has said as much.

In that way, we are a perfect fit.

The more I got to know him, even now as I write this, I recognize that Chris is *the* prayer answered. There have been signs, like when his name comes up in conversation, people gush and say, "That guy was a real shit-magnet cop, but he's a damn good man!"

I was at a Pat Tillman event, and I ran into Maricopa Country's Sheriff Penzone. I handed him a Love Note and when I mentioned Chris' name, he smiled wide. The two worked together years ago.

"Chris is a good man," Penzone said.

A good man.

That's when I knew Chris was the one for me. He *is* the "good man" I had been praying for. Sheriff Penzone said it himself, and his endorsement was good enough for me.

After Chris showered that morning, he stepped out of the bathroom smelling like soap and spearmint. He had on a fresh pair of slacks and a blue, button-up shirt. I pretended not to notice, as I watched him lumber into the room, fumbling with a blue silk necktie. I buried my smile beneath the blankets. I couldn't tell if he was attempting a Windsor knot or a noose.

"Let me," I said, crawling out of bed.

Chris, more than a half of a foot taller than me, blushed and turned his back to me. I am pretty sure he expected me to tie his tie from behind, like a father would for his young (much smaller) son. However, without a step ladder or a bean to grow a magic beanstalk, that wasn't happening.

"Ummm ..." I giggled. "You're going to have to turn around and face me."

Looking a little sheepish, Chris did an about-face, and I got to work on my best Windsor knot.

"Make it skinny," he said.

"Skinny?"

"Yes. That knot looks too fat."

"Are you calling me fat?" I asked, giving him *the* look.

"No. I'm calling your knot fat."

As I attempted to tie a "skinny" knot, I felt his eyes on me. I was standing there in my pajamas. He was in his business suit, and we were in a hotel room somewhere in San Diego—together, just one day after I had returned from a week in California. The whole thing felt surreal. I hardly knew this man, but there we were, tying a "skinny" necktie for the big interview, a job that would, ultimately, take him from me. The truth was we hadn't even kissed yet, but the way we bantered back and forth and the easiness of our conversation, you would have thought we had been together for years.

"It's too fat," he said, looking in the mirror.

"What do you mean … 'too fat'?"

"It looks like a clown tie!" he countered, sticking his forefinger through the loop between the collar and the knot and tugging at it.

"A wide knot exudes confidence," I insisted.

"Yeah, if you're Bozo!"

Damn those dimples.

"Beggars can't be choosers, Bozo!"

In the end, I tied the skinniest, (fat!) knot in all of clown-necktie history, and I sent the good man on his way. A few hours later, on the ride back to Arizona, the call came. Chris got the job. You should have seen the excitement in his face. He was beyond elated. It meant he was (finally!) moving to the beach—his lifelong dream. For me, it was bittersweet. If I am being honest; it sucked! While I was seriously happy for him, I couldn't help but feel sad. Once again, I was being left behind. Not realizing it, I sighed out loud. That was just me resigning myself to friendship, even though

I was starting to feel a whole lot more than that.

"You're welcome," I said, as he hung up the phone.

"For what?" he asked.

"For getting you the job with my fat necktie."

He chuckled.

I feigned a giggle, then turned my gaze from him to the passenger side window. Trying *not* to think about another hard goodbye, I watched the desert landscape roll by, as we listened to Van Morrison croon, "*Mama told me there'd be days like this,*" on satellite radio.

Days like this, indeed.

My husband and I received your letter today. It was an honor to be remembered by someone who has a heart as big as yours. God bless you. Thank you for restoring my heart in our America.

—Denise M., U.S. Veteran Spouse

TWENTY-EIGHT
The First Kiss

Where your story begins has very little bearing on where it will end. I believe that with my whole heart. I was born a small-town girl in Gallup, New Mexico, a stone's throw from Route 66 in 1968. There wasn't much happening in those parts, if you don't count the time when I was battling a bad case of bronchitis as a baby. Mom, being a first-time mother, rushed me to the local ER. As we lingered in the waiting room, she couldn't help but notice the man seated directly across from us. It was Johnny Cash!

The man in black.

Now, I have led a charmed life, but *that* is nothing short of the coolest thing—**EVER**! My point being, there will be some moments in your life that will knock your socks off, moments you have very little control over, like sitting next to Johnny Cash in a hospital waiting room. And, while those moments are notable, there will be times in your life that will call for courage, and if you find it in yourself to answer the call … be prepared to blow your own mind!

I'm serious!

Life is a culmination of decisions—big and small, good and bad, right and wrong. Sometimes these decisions must be carefully thought through and other times, a girl has got to just go with her gut and do that thing she knows in her heart she must do—no matter how scared she is or whether or not she's got anyone in her corner rooting for her.

If you never go, you will never know.

It was six o'clock on a Friday night. I was debating whether or not to text message Chris. We had spent the better part of a few weeks working tirelessly on his manuscript and, occasionally, hiking Thunderbird Mountain. On top of which, we had recently returned from a road trip together to San Diego for his job interview. It was abundantly clear that I enjoyed his company, and I got the feeling he enjoyed mine, so (after much deliberation) I decided to take a chance and invite him over to my place for a night in— Chinese takeout and a DVD.

I had a serious case of butterflies. Despite the fact I had already seen this man in his boxer briefs in the early morning hours, I was going to have to muster some serious courage. This was hard for me, a real stretch. It meant going out on a limb. I would be bringing this man into my home and, quite possibly, into my heart, which, if you think about it, was sort of foolish since he was clearly on his way to California. As his "book editor lady," the woman programmed into this man's cell phone as ***Book Girl Natalie***, I was all for keeping things professional. However, I couldn't ignore the fact that there was something special happening here.

Seeing as it was after six o'clock on a Friday night, it was quite possible Chris was already out for the evening, which would make sense and would make my mooning a moot point. My heart was pounding hard inside my chest—fast, like the resting heart rate of a worried rabbit. I perched myself at the edge of the sofa, staring intently at the blinking blue cursor in an open text message. Taking advice straight out of Chris' manuscript and Lt. Col. Dave Grossman's Killology philosophy, I took a combat breath: Four counts in—hold four counts—four counts out.

"What are you waiting for," I exhaled, tapping out an invite.

Book Girl Natalie
Feel like some Chinese takeout and a DVD tonight?

I held my breath for a couple of seconds, and then ...

Chris Hoyer
On my way! Put in the food order. I'll pick it up.

The man responded without hesitation, and he landed at my doorstep with Chinese takeout in one hand and a selection of DVDs in the other—in under thirty minutes.

Impressive!

Which is kind of funny because the man lived way across town. I guess the manager training program at Domino's Pizza all those years ago paid off.

Thirty minutes, indeed!

Love walked into my life with a slow swagger, sporting a pair of old, cowboy boots, washed-out blue jeans and a Glock .45 tucked into the small of his back. I felt it when we hugged, both the affection and his sidearm. Relieving him of the Chinese takeout and DVD assortment, Chris pulled the loaded firearm from his waistband and laid it onto the pony wall in my entryway. That was a first, and I'm not going to lie. It was kind of hot!

When he showed up at my front door that night with a four o'clock shadow and a dimpled smile, I still wasn't convinced that God had, indeed, delivered on His promise. I mean, the man was leaving for California any day, and we hadn't even kissed.

As soon as he sat down on the living room sofa, Danni, the neurotic of my two cats, landed in Chris' lap. This was a sign, an act of God assuring me that this might be *the* man because this cat never, *ever* shows her face when there's company. Danni, a rescue, was abused as a kitten, her tail broken and healed up into the shape of a pretzel. Except for me and my youngest son, she trusts no one and remains a phantom most of the time. I watched in awe as Chris gently massaged her ears, not appreciating the minor miracle of the cat kneading his chest. It was a match made in Heaven.

Clearly there was something about Chris, but he wasn't at all what I was expecting. I was still sort of caught up in the idea that he hired me to edit his book. That gig, in and of itself, was a blessing—a gift. The fact that he turned out to be a "good man," someone who instantly won the favor of *the* most phobic feline on the planet, was the gravy.

Who said animals don't have a sixth sense about people?

Around the time Mom was battling her disease, Chris was navigating the post-traumatic stress brought on by a twenty-year career as a street cop. He had survived the worst of the worst, including a wicked gunfight in his eighteenth year. At the time it was a faraway idea that such terrible things could happen in the world, that good men and women could die in an effort to protect and serve their community. With my firstborn son taking on this new career, the idea was hitting closer to home.

One of the things I appreciated most about Chris was that he was a real gentleman. He took his time getting to know me. When it took the man six hours (and one classic B movie) to screw up the courage to kiss me that night, I knew in my heart and in that warm, wet kiss that it was the start of something epic. As he leaned in, I remember hoping that first kiss would be good because, as every girl knows, the first kiss sets the tone. I was rooting for him in my head. I think Danni was, too. And he nailed it!

Since that first kiss, I have not been able to shake him, not from my mind, my heart or my side. He is the one for me. With the exception of the accompanying box fan, Chris is a badass blend of Mad Max and Neil Peart, with just enough Tim Allen in him to make him fun to be around. I know Mom would have loved him. Even though our perspective on love differed, and she was never fully on board with my dating as a single mom, I think she would have given Chris her blessing. Something tells me, like Danni, she already has.

A few weeks ago, I took my son to the movies. When we returned to my truck, I found a note on my truck addressed to a combat veteran. As I skeptically opened the letter and read it, I was completely taken aback by the heartfelt message. I was literally at a loss for words. Not only was it handwritten, but very inspirational and touching. Your letter came at the most perfect time too, as I was having a very rough week. Not only did this brighten my day, but it made my month. As I posted it on Facebook, it didn't take long for the internet sleuths to find you. Your letter is proudly displayed on the door of my fridge, along with my six-year-old son's drawings. When I look at it, I take it to heart, knowing that there are people like you that take the time out of your day to brighten other's day. From the bottom of my heart, thank you, Natalie, for everything you do.

—LeRoy S., Combat Veteran

TWENTY-NINE

The Vietnam Veteran

O f all the ink we've injected into the hearts of our nation's heroes over the past five years, it's the Vietnam Veteran who takes the cake. It's no secret I have a soft spot for them, as they are the ones who felt the draft—literally and figuratively. Many were drafted into the war, and all of them felt the (political) draft coming out of it. These veterans, whether they saw combat or not, were in a no-win situation, much like our law enforcement officers today, scorned for doing what they had to do, what most anyone else would not dare do for the sake of the greater good.

For every conversation I've had with a Vietnam Veteran, whether in a parking lot, in the frozen food aisle of the grocery store or while standing in line at a local coffee shop, it's the same story, different man. It always begins with the unwelcomed homecoming, having to change out of their military uniform behind the scenes at the airport, so as to avoid the torment of war protestors.

One US Navy Veteran, a man named Peter, teared up as he told me that he had no idea of the violence and protests going on back home. It wasn't until he stepped off of the ship in his dress whites that he realized what was happening. Having survived a tour in Vietnam, an agitated protestor chucked a hot cup of coffee at him, staining his freshly pressed uniform, but that's not what hurt. It was the hateful rhetoric being spewed and spit in his face by people who had no idea what he had been through, nor did they care. Peter, all these years later, bowed his head and with wet eyes, said, "I was serving my country, and they hated me for it."

Candidly sharing these painful experiences with a stranger invokes deep-seated emotion in our veterans—young and old. However, there seems to be a small degree of healing when they are handed a Love Note. Oftentimes, it sparks conversation, giving these men and women a chance to get some of the bad stuff off their chest. This was an unforeseen benefit of our mission. Who could have predicted we'd open up such an important conversation?

The way I see it, our veterans are the keepers of our security and freedom. I have learned more about this great country from conversations with these guys in parking lots than I have in any classroom or book. Moreover, it has been the great privilege of my life to hold these warriors in my arms as their tears catch up to them.

Honestly, there are days I wonder if we deserve them, those who dare put on a uniform to do what the better part of the population would not (or could not) do and then stand and be judged for it by those who have no idea how ugly the world can be. George Orwell summed up these warriors best when he said, "*People sleep peaceably in their beds at night only because rough men stand ready to do violence on their behalf.*"

Orwell got it right.

And, so, the best thing we can do in return for these warriors is simply lend them our ear and, perhaps, even a shoulder. With the exception of the words, "Thank you" and "Welcome home," there is nothing more to say.

I've looked enough of these warriors in the eye to know that they do their level best to bear the burden, themselves, so as not to saddle their friends and family with the crushing load that comes with war and combat. More often than not, they have much to absolve, of themselves and of others, and the bended ear of a stranger allows for a small piece of that.

I'm always amazed at how easy it is to rouse these big, strong combat warriors into opening their hearts about the things that hurt. A simple Love Note can do that. It helps in the healing—for our combat veterans, for people like me, and for the world at large.

The Purple Heart is a United States military decoration awarded in the name of the president to those wounded or killed while serving their country. Because of a Love Note, I've met a few Purple Hearts, but there is one who stands out above the rest. His name is Roger.

I left Roger a Love Note somewhere in the beginning of our little mission. It was a cloudy day, and Mom and I were patrolling the Scottsdale parking lot for veteran plates. Roger's car had Purple

Heart plates, and it was parked in front of a Vietnamese restaurant. Don't ask me how I remember every little detail of these deliveries. I just do.

I'm sort of a savant when it comes to Love Notes.

The parking lot was packed, so I had to park a few rows away and hoof it. As I approached his car, I reached into my purse and found a note addressed specifically to a Purple Heart. Checking my surroundings, as it is always a bit awkward putting stuff on people's cars, I tucked the note under the windshield wiper and vamoosed. I still get giddy at the thought.

Two months later, I received a message from the Purple Heart. It read: *"I received a note on my car in Scottsdale from you a couple of months ago. At the time, I was in a dark moment, so you really made my day. I shared this note with hundreds of my fellow vets on LinkedIn and Facebook because it belongs to all of them. Thank you so much. Keep up the good work and God Bless!!"*

I responded to Roger, and he opened up to me about his days in Nam, sharing the story of his youth. Come to find, after college, he couldn't wait for the draft, so he voluntarily enlisted in the US Army.

Yes! You read me right.

It wasn't long before he was shipped out to Vietnam where he spent most of 1969. Because he had a college education, he could have served as an officer, but Roger refused. He often teases, "I didn't want to be an officer. I would rather be shot from the front than the back."

So, he was infantry and became wounded on a search and destroy mission on St. Patrick's Day in '69, earning him the Purple Heart. If you ask him about it, he'll tell you, "I'm not Irish, but I sure was lucky that day. My platoon sergeant, my leader, was standing next to me. He got the bulk of the explosion. He died on the spot."

Roger has become a special part of our Love Note story, not to mention a very important part of my life. The first time we met in person was at the Pat Tillman Run in Tempe, Arizona in  2018. He invited me to meet him at the finish line, which I did. We were instant friends. He has since shared with me the traumas that followed him home from Vietnam and told how the images from that war still haunt him to this day. Again, I have learned so much more about the history of our country from talking with our veterans than I have from school—kindergarten to college.

Roger is a big believer in our little Love Note mission. He writes them all the time and leaves them for veterans almost everywhere he goes. Every now and then he'll reach out and tell me all about it. Sometimes he sends photographs of the Love Notes he leaves on veterans' cars. Next to the greeting cards he sends me in the mail every Mother's Day, those text messages, emails and photos are some of my favorite correspondence. It's so nice when friends are thinking of you while they are out spreading love. In a small way, it means you are a part of it, an accomplice to it. And, sometimes, you are right there in the thick of it.

Guilty as charged.

A few years ago, Roger invited me to the Phoenix VA to hand out Love Notes with him. We literally combed the hallways together, handing out dozens of notes of handwritten gratitude. Roger would playfully antagonize the old sailors with his favorite chant, "Go Army! Beat Navy!"

That was fun!

Roger can always be counted on to give back. In the nine consecutive years he has participated in the Annual Pat's Run, he and his supporters have invested over $40,000 in college scholarships for many of our nation's veterans and active military personnel. He often brings up the fact that he, himself, couldn't have completed his college education without the help of scholarships and student loans.

I accompanied Roger to a Pat Tillman Foundation event in 2019, the same night I met Sheriff Penzone. Roger was in his element, speaking words of encouragement to the scholarship recipients and Marie, Tillman's widow. And every now and then, in Roger fashion, he'd needle a Navy man, "Go Army! Beat Navy!"

It's funny how life works. When you find your purpose, you find your people. And when that happens, nothing is impossible!

Welcome home, Roger That!

Hey! My name is Chris, and you guys left a note on my car the other day. That particular day was a really hard day for me. I was feeling pretty low. Your note made my day and brought me back up to where I wanted to be. I just wanted to let you know how much I appreciate your kindness and thoughtfulness. People like you are the reason I am proud to have been able to serve my country, and people like you are the reason I am continuing to pursue a public service career. Thank you for what you are doing. I mean that from the very bottom of my heart. Thank you.

——Chris O., U.S. Military Veteran

THIRTY

Another Hard Goodbye

I was heartbroken. Chris was leaving Arizona for California—forever. The night before he left, he stopped by my house for what turned out to be *the* fastest goodbye in history—quicker than a McDonald's drive-thru. I had been working all day with Carol, editing her book and sharing a beautiful, homecooked meal on her terrace that overlooked Fountain Hills. As wonderful as that day (and that view) was, it was eclipsed by the dreaded goodbye waiting for me that afternoon.

Did I mention I am bad at goodbye?

Chris and I planned to meet at my place later that day. So, after a late lunch, I kissed Carol on the cheek and rushed home. I jumped into a hot, bubble bath and braced for impact. As I stepped out of the big basin, Chris texted that he was pulling up to my house. That's when I heard the loud, rumble of his big, diesel truck.

OMG! He was early!

My hair was soaking wet. I barely had time to throw myself together—tank top, shorts, no shoes, and the quickest makeup transformation ever! My heart was racing the whole time. I had no idea how this would play out or that it would even pan out.

Just breathe.

As soon as I opened the front door, Chris jerked his chin in the direction of his truck and then turned and walked away—not even the requisite hello and how are you?

"So, it's going to be like that," I whispered.

Here we go.

Knees quivering, I followed along behind him, feigning the faintest smile. I don't remember much, except him opening his arms up and me being sucked into him, like a black hole. The pull was so strong, I couldn't escape, even if I tried. Maybe it was just because he was leaving, but suddenly everything seemed so clear. Box fan or no box fan, I was beginning to fall for this man. It wasn't as though I didn't come with two (furry) box fans of my own, disguised as tuxedo cats named Danni and Bella.

*Do not cry. Do **not** cry.*

He lifted my chin with his finger and pressed his warm lips to mine. I don't remember us saying much, but I do remember him turning toward his truck and opening up the back door. He reached in and pulled out his favorite hometown sweatshirt that read: Portsmouth. As he turned around to face me, clutching the faded blue sweatshirt I had bargained for in the book deal, my lip began to quiver, and my eyes began to water.

"It's yours," he said.

I just about lost it. Burying my face into his chest, I wanted to ask, *The sweatshirt or your heart?* I couldn't. I kept those words to myself, hidden deep. I had a feeling I knew the answer, but I couldn't say for sure. All I knew was that it wasn't the time or the place to get in the way. The man was on his way out of town, chasing his life's dream of living by the beach. I was not about to be *that* girl, the one to give him pause, to hold him back. I knew he wanted this new life more than anything, and so I wanted it for him, almost as much. At the same time, I was *just* starting to like the dude. The feeling I was feeling was so unexpected, and as much as I wanted to root for "us," I wouldn't put myself through another long-distance relationship—I couldn't.

As Chris kissed me goodbye and literally drove off into the sunset, I felt a tugging at my heart. In less time than it takes to order a coffee at Starbucks, he was gone, and I was left standing there, curbside, parting gift in hand. It was the worst. I went back inside, slipped into his ginormous sweatshirt and cried. I immediately called my brother on the telephone. In between sobs and snivels, I gasped, "He's gone. He leaves for California at dawn."

As I tried catching my breath, Nate smiled. I could actually hear his smirk through the phone line.

"Dude," he said. "Go with him."

"What?!" I replied, stiffening my spine and wiping my eyes with the sleeve of my new sweatshirt.

"Living by the beach is what you've always dreamed of," he said. "And, besides that ... he's the one for you, Nat."

I couldn't believe my ears, not just because Nate was being so blunt, but because it sounded so reminiscent of what Mom might say in such a moment. She was nothing if not a cup half full of clarity in times like these. On top of which, Nate hadn't even met Chris.

"I'm serious, sissy. I knew it from the first time I saw you two together in that selfie you sent me. Chris is the one! I told Jen the same thing on the night you sent that photo."

"Really?"

"Yes. What are the chances of meeting someone who has the exact same dream as you? I knew just looking at the two of you that this was meant to be. The timing is perfect. You have nothing holding you here. It's now or never, Nat."

For the better part of my life, I did what I thought was right for everyone I loved—and I would do it all again, but Nate was right. I had nothing holding me back. I was falling in love with this man, and he was headed for a life I had always dreamed of, which makes me wonder if the Universe wasn't trying to tell me something.

It was as if a carrot was dangling in front of my face. And at the same time, it was way too soon to be chasing this man to California. I wasn't *that* girl. I'm far too reserved to make such a bold move, another "gift" I inherited from my mother. Besides, we had only spent two and a half months together, mostly on a professional basis. While romance was blossoming, albeit at a snail's pace, it was too new to know for sure. What I did know for sure was that I was just beginning to enjoy the magic that comes in getting to know someone more intimately. It had been a long time since I had felt that particular tickle of butterflies in my belly, and now that tickle felt more like an ulcer.

Ah, snap!

I cried myself to sleep that night in the comfort and warmth of Chris' sweatshirt. It was all quite dramatic for the girl who, like her late mother, usually does her crying in the rain, and who, in the end, almost always gets her "goat."

At least Chris and I still had work left to do on the book. That was something and so was our friendship. Some people come into our life for a reason, and I had no doubt Chris had come into mine for something special. If the book were the sole point of our meeting, it would have been more than I could have ever asked for, professionally speaking. And, so, I simply thanked God that night for Chris, and every night that followed, praying that he find the life he was searching for.

Early the next morning, on the drive to San Diego, Chris reached out, inviting me to visit him that weekend. He was barely out of the Phoenix city limits, and he was already thinking about me.

"Bring my sweatshirt," he teased. "It's 59 degrees in Cali."

My heart melted.

"I'll be there."

Over the next few months, I made several trips to visit Chris in San Diego—by way of airplane and automobile. We spent more time that summer having fun and getting to know one another than we did editing his book. Chris is always so eager to get outdoors. We would take long walks together along the beach and up and down Neptune Avenue, our favorite beachside neighborhood in Encinitas. He tried teaching me how to surf, and I almost had to drive him to the ER for stitches at the end of the lesson. We went on a hunt to find the best street tacos and beer, which was a crapshoot, until we discovered City Tacos. Chris would put me on the back of his CBR 1000, and we'd zip up to the mountains or to Long Beach. Mom would have hated me riding on the back of a crouch rocket.

Somewhere out there, she is shaking her head.

The truth was, Chris and I were both in our element, and it felt right being together. He wooed me with flowers and gifts, and surprised me in little, off-the-wall ways. And I fed him healthy, homecooked meals and, ultimately, accepted the box fan as a part of the package because Chris was someone I could see myself with. Even the ways in which we were polar opposites seemed to work for us. He, being Mr. Manly, and me, being fiercely feminine, sparked a strong intimate connection, unlike anything I've ever known. Forget the fact that Chris still operates in cop mode. Being the quintessential protector, he is logical to a fault and routine/detail oriented. While I, on the other hand, wander around with my head in the clouds, and always, (always!) unable to find my reading glasses. He razzes me about this, and to this day, I tease that he is as much my secret service detail as he is my boyfriend.

In all seriousness, Chris and I were having the time of our lives. However, we hadn't yet said those three little words—I love you. I could feel them lingering in the back of every kiss good morning and goodbye, which made matters even more confusing. Being an introvert, there were days when I would go quiet and introspective for hours at a time. Chris is patient, so he never pushed me to talk. We would walk along the beach for miles without saying a word, as I mulled over where this was going. The truth was, aside from having to pick up my life and move to California, there was the matter of Chris' marital status. He had been separated for five years, and because he never spoke of making it official, I couldn't see carrying on without him tying up that rather large loose end, for everyone's sake. Even though his marriage had ended, I could see he felt bound by the commitment, itself, but still ... how can a man move forward when he is still coupled to his past?

As the summer drew to a close, it was only getting harder to say goodbye. I began to dread Sundays, my favorite day of the week, because it meant a curbside farewell at the airport. With each sendoff, I knew that I was either going to have to breakup with this guy or pick up and move to California. Only one of those options seemed plausible, so I started giving serious thought to putting my house up for sale.

Natalie, anyone who has talent, like you do, is a lucky girl. I know the BIG one is still out there, and you are a true magnet. I'm also a lucky girl to have been given a daughter with so much love of words because you know how I love to read. We will just "keep swimming" and making a difference to others. What greater task than that? Keep your chin up. (Your partner in crime! Ha!)

—Mom, 2013

THIRTY-ONE

Home Stretch

F eeling inordinately brave, I mentioned the idea of selling my house to Chris in passing. I remember it being a cool, cloudy afternoon in late June 2019. We were ambling around downtown Encinitas, walking off a rather large portion of *the* most delicious tacos I had ever had in my life. I teased about flying home and selling my crib, and even though it was probably the sangria talking, it felt good to say it out loud because I knew the Universe was eavesdropping.

"I would love that more than anything, Nat," Chris smiled. "But don't do it for me. If you do this, pick up your life in Arizona and move to California, do it for you. Do it because it's what you always dreamed of as a kid."

I was so happy to hear him say that because this move was important to me, not just because this good man landed there first, but because *it was* what I had always wanted. Moving to the beach was *the* dream, and if I did it for any other reason, it left too much room for doubt and disappointment. If I made the move for me, come what may, I could look myself in the mirror and say, "You did it, girl!" It was in that conversation, on that *very* sidewalk along Highway 101, that I knew I had to do it. I had to do the brave thing and follow my heart. It was all leading up to this, all of it—Mom, the mentors, the mission, the man. It was all becoming so clear.

When I first began contemplating moving to California, I was scared to death. I had no idea how I would make it happen. Because our lives are determined by the decisions we make, big and small, I was petrified of making the wrong one, plus I no longer had my corner man (Mom!) to cheer me on. I kid you not. I was actively inventing excuses **not** to make the move. It just seemed easier to stick with what I knew, even though it was a life that no longer fit.

I came up with some of *the* most ridiculous excuses. Topping the list, in no particular order: 1.) I did not want to inconvenience my cats, as if cats aren't predisposed to feel inconvenienced, 2.) I would have to deal with California's terrible freeway system and gas prices, and 3.) Chris is a junk-food-eating machine. I had never seen anything like it.

I know what you're thinking, but these were real concerns.

The truth was I had nothing to lose. My life, at that point, was a whole lot less complicated than it had been in decades. I had been liberated as both an empty nester and as a caregiver. On top of which, as I mentioned before, it was not for me to figure out the how and the why. It was only for me to have "faith the size of a mustard seed." All that aside, I was being a worrier, not warrior, and the thing that kept me up at night was not that I might fail. We all fail sometimes. What kept me up at night was that if Mom, the strongest woman I knew, could die, then none of us was getting out of this alive. It was only a matter of time, and since I had more summers behind me than ahead of me, why would I make excuses *not* to go with my gut and make this move to California?

It was the beach, not Baghdad!

If you've spent any amount of time in a room full of cancer patients receiving chemotherapy, you know that life is worth fighting for. Once a week for almost two years I drove Mom to her treatments, and while I can't say that I know what it feels like to ingest that toxic cocktail, I can tell you that I will never forget the pure awfulness of its effects, which is why I believe one should not wait to get sick before deciding to do those things that make them happy. Every day that I wake up with air in my lungs, feeling healthy and strong, I am grateful to God. And, so, I knew there was no excuse good enough to chicken out.

Life is big, beautiful and messy. And it's just waiting for someone like me (and you) to step up and do the brave thing. Life should be something to write home about, and our mistakes should not be something to fear, but rather something to revel in because it means we are trying. On top of which, our mistakes are the price we pay for a full and happy life—period, end of story.

When I think back to those days and weeks I spent sitting at Mom's bedside, when nothing seemed to be going right, I never could have imagined that it would have led me to this enchanting time in my life. Mom was right. God, did, indeed, have bigger plans for me. I just didn't have a clue what that could look like. Honestly, it turned out to be so much more amazing than even I could have dreamed. I certainly never anticipated falling in love at the end of that long, hard road. Now, there's a home truth, considering how hard I had been praying for a "good man."

Danielle and my brother, on the other hand, knew that Chris was the one for me, even before he and I knew. They must have seen something in the two of us. In fact, every time I tried talking myself out of Chris, Danielle would step up and say, "Stop it! He loves you!"

And, as for everyone else in my life, falling in love with Chris and making the decision to move to California was a HUGE surprise. Elise didn't even see it coming. She texted me one day, curious to see if Chris and I were officially a "thing." When I confirmed it, she lit up like a Christmas tree!

Conversely, after learning about Chris and me, Jane fell off the map. I tried reaching out to her a couple of times, but never received a response. I can respect that. At the same time, I hope she knows how much I love and appreciate her part in our love story. Chris and I would never have met, had it not been for Jane, our mutual (and sweet) friend. I will always be grateful to her for that and for believing in my mission.

Not long after Chris moved to San Diego, I ran with a group of firefighters in the April 2019 Pat Tillman Run in Tempe, Arizona.

I met these firefighters (Brad, Josue, Sergio and Nik) the year before when I greeted Roger, the Purple Heart, at the finish line. I use the word "met" lightly, since I didn't actually see their faces or speak to them directly. They were all geared up from head to toe in turnouts and oxygen tanks, each wearing a mask that covered their entire face. Approaching them was a bit intimidating, as the masks were screen prints of scary skulls or something to that effect. They called themselves "Team Bad Axes." After they crossed the finish line, a large group of people gathered around them, taking photographs with them and patting them on the back for having run the race in full gear. After summoning the courage, I pushed through the crowd and handed each firefighter a Love Note.

Months later, one of the firefighters, a good guy named Brad, reached out to me via my Nothing but Love Notes Facebook page. He asked me to run with "Team Bad Axes" in 2019 in the Annual Pat Tillman Run, which I did. To be honest, I was a little worried about "running" 4.2 miles with guys much younger than me, but I was promised the pace would be relative to that of a snail. I'm not going to lie, as a woman flirting with fifty, it was of some comfort to be running with first responders, if you know what I mean. This was yet another shot for me to step outside the box, to run alongside those everyday heroes who put themselves in the line of fire for the sake of their community. It was also a good way for me to build up the confidence I needed to move forward in this little adventure. And, if nothing else, I got to dole out lots of Love Notes along the way.

Once again, I was a part of something special, something bigger than me. On top of which, I was honored that these firefighters would even think to ask me to be a part of their "race." Maybe this movement mattered more than Mom and I originally thought.

In the home stretch of the race, the firefighters were invited up on stage to interview with a local news anchor. They insisted I join them, and somehow Nothing but Love Notes got its day in the sun—again. I believe it was Brad who threw in the shameless plug, promoting our little mission on television. It always surprises me just how much affection one little Love Note can get, especially from the strong, silent types.

A few months later, in the middle of July, I hired a kid named Geordan to sell my house. I only call him a kid because he went to high school with my oldest son Billy. They played football together. The reason I chose to hire him was because of a handwritten note. He wrote me a (professional) Love Note on a postcard, offering his services as a realtor. Even though I wasn't in the market at the time, I was moved by the handwritten correspondence and kept it in a junk drawer for almost a year.

It was a paperclip, of sorts.

My house sold in just twelve days. I didn't expect it to go so fast. On one hand, I wasn't ready. On the other hand, I had been waiting for this my *whole* life. Within one month I had given away most of my belongings. I packed up the little that was left into a handful of boxes, tucked them into a U-Haul and headed west with Chris in the driver's seat.

My two cats were in traveling kennels in the center console, and I was in the passenger seat, nervously nursing a strawberry refresher (no berries). I finally had money in the bank and a whole new path to carve out for myself. I sound brave, but you should have seen me the night before.

As my youngest son, Alec and his buddy Caleb, helped Chris and my brother load the U-Haul with my things, I was freaking out. In my head, I was screaming, "I'm not going! I can't do this!"

Forget the fact that I was homeless at the time.

It was all so surreal. I couldn't believe what was happening. Was I really going to leave Arizona, a place I had lived for most of my life, to live out my days next to the California coast? Where my rent would be more than triple my mortgage payment? I mean, I had hoped it would happen one day, living the life of a writer by the beach—warm, golden sunshine on my face and sand in my toes. I just never dreamed it would be at this place in my life … with the man sitting next to me, a man who, unbeknownst to me, lived less than a mile away from me twenty years ago.

Who knew?

I wish I could say that I did. All I knew is that being with Chris felt a whole lot like holding a warm load of laundry in my arms—fresh from the dryer or slipping into my favorite boyfriend blue jeans on day two of wearing them. I just wanted to curl up in him and take a nap. He made me feel safe, warm and, above all things, loved.

When we first started dating, Chris admitted that he was afraid of falling in love with me. He didn't want to find himself in the same situation as relationships past. He also said that he wasn't the kind of guy to hold hands with a girl. I thought it was kind of strange, but I didn't say much. I figured if he wanted to be with me and hold my hand, he would and, eventually, he did.

That's got to mean something, right?

So, now when Chris holds my hand, which is quite often, I have to smile. That sweet, simple gesture triggers something in me that I cannot put into words, except to say that when I am with him, I am home, and it couldn't have less to do with living alongside the California coast.

As we pulled into San Diego on September 7, 2019, the "big move" felt rather anti-climactic. It certainly wasn't as hard as I thought it would be, let alone scary. And to think, I almost let fear get in the way. I literally almost talked myself out of it ... out of him. However, as it turned out, the dream was nothing more than a short five-hour drive away and a brand-new zip code.

I had a very long and annoying ass day today. I'm tired, hungry and in desperate need of a hot shower. But then this amazing-ass shit happened. When I finally got back to the workshop and headed to my car to go home, I found this letter in my window. I don't know who this person is and have no clue how they knew I was a vet, but whoever you are, thank you. You turned a shitty day into an awesome one. You put a smile on my face and restored my faith in humanity just a little bit today. And, considering everything that has happened lately, and what this upcoming weekend is all about, I really fuckin' appreciate that. So, from the bottom of my heart, thank you, kind stranger.

—Kevin H., U.S. Military Veteran

THIRTY-TWO

All the Way

With warm, wet lips, Chris bent over the bed and kissed me goodbye. I opened my sleepy eyes to find him freshly showered, shaved and outfitted in his instructor's uniform. He smelled good, like soap and cedar—odeur de homme. He looked good, too. Better up close than long distance. It was the easiest goodbye we had navigated in a long time.

"Make yourself at home," he said, as he headed out the front door for work, leaving me warm and contented under the covers.

It was my fifth official day in California—a Wednesday. I lay there, wondering what would come of this big move. The plan was for me and my two neurotic cats to stay with him for a few days, until I got situated into an apartment in Oceanside. Again, I didn't want to rush things with Chris. Good things take time. I wondered if this move would make things weird, but Chris seemed ecstatic and welcoming of all three of us. He gave us complete run of the place. That tiny beachside apartment, albeit small, felt good, like home.

That morning, I ran to the grocery store for a few things. When I got back to Chris' place, I started prepping for dinner—

cheeseburgers. What I wasn't prepped for was finding photo prints of Chris and another woman tucked under a stack of mail on the kitchen table while making room for a cutting board. I could tell it was recent because 1.) He had the beard, and 2.) It was on our beach—a sunset selfie with some broad I had never seen before.

Of all the nerve.

I knew he had a lot of friends visiting him that summer, but he never mentioned this woman to me. I didn't know the full story, but it triggered something in me, old wounds from relationships past. I had been here before, and even though it had been decades since something like that had ever happened, I went into autopilot. My heart sank, and my head instantly began devising an exit strategy. It was all I could do to pack up my stuff and get out of there without falling to pieces.

Even though Chris and I weren't officially "together," and we had never talked (respectively) about "us" as a couple, seeing those photos wrecked me. Time stopped. My hands trembled. I sat down, took a deep breath and picked up the telephone. I called the leasing agent at my apartment-to-be complex and asked if there was any way I could move in *that* day. Of course, there was a long, laundry list of things I needed to accomplish before that could happen, including setting up electricity, submitting bank records in lieu of paystubs, obtaining a money order for the deposit and getting my cats vaccinated—to name a few. I also needed to dump the rental and buy a new car, but I would save that for another day.

Ugh.

It was ten o'clock in the morning, and because Chris' truck was in the shop, he would be expecting a ride home at five that afternoon. I didn't have much time to waste, so I quickly put the burger fixings in the fridge, packed up my stuff and loaded it into the rental car. I nearly pulled my back out getting one cat out from the far reaches of Chris' closet and the other out from underneath his big, ugly couch. They were stressing out, sensing another move. It's amazing what you can accomplish with a little adrenaline surge.

Meanwhile, Chris had been calling and texting all day long. I didn't have the heart nor the stomach to respond. I simply packed up my things, cleaned up his place, as if me and the cats had never been there, leaving the photos (and my copy of his apartment key) in plain sight on the kitchen table. It was all I could do to get myself and my animals into an apartment before dark. Like me, Chris would have to find his own way home.

Later that night I curled up on the bedroom floor of my new apartment. I was wrapped up in an enormous, pink, knit blanket that I purchased at Target an hour earlier. I lay there in the dark, digesting a peanut butter and jelly sandwich, the only thing I had eaten all day. My cats were freaking out, hiding in dark places. Danni was curled up at my feet under the covers and Bella was underneath the kitchen sink.

We were all feeling a little skittish.

The moonlight poured in through my patio sliding door. It was of little comfort to me, as I cried into my brand-new pillow. I was feeling a little lost, unsure of what to do next. However, I wasn't sorry. I was in California, further from family, but closer to everything I had always dreamed of. At about nine o'clock that night, after walking eight miles and then Ubering the remainder of the way home from work, Chris texted.

Chris Hoyer

A few things you need to know: I am (and have been) 100% faithful to you and will be if we stay together. You did NOT make a mistake getting close to me. I will fight to keep us together if that's what you want. That is DEFINITELY what I want. I am not seeing anyone but you. You can trust me. I won't expect to hear from you for a couple of days, but will you let me know whatever is going on? Please.

I read the text message several times before I was finally able to close my eyes and fall asleep. I did not respond. I did not know how to respond. I tend to shut down in situations like this. I go dark. I know that's not a good thing, but I'm an introvert and that's what we do. The more I thought about it, the sicker to my stomach I got. That's when I knew. I was in love with this man.

The next day, I was in a tizzy, only about another female. Somewhere in the process of moving in, I lost Bella. I thought she might have freaked out and jumped from our second story balcony. The apartment was only 780 square feet, so there were only so many places she could hide, especially since there was no furniture. I called out to her, but she didn't come to me.

I panicked. I knew she had to be lost because Bella is a lot like a dog. Every time I call out to her or walk through the front door, she is there to greet me. I had walked in the front door several times that morning and got no greeting—no nothing. I started looking for her outside, walking around the large complex, calling out to her. The leasing agent had warned that there were a lot of coyote sightings in the area, which made me feel completely guilty for bringing her all the way to California just to become brunch for Wile E. Coyote. In less than a week, I had lost the boy and now Bella.

Not a great start!

After a few hours of combing the complex, praying to God I find my girl, I ambled back to my apartment, chin dragging. As I walked through the front door, for the tenth time that morning, Bella skulked out from the laundry closet. When she saw me, she stretched into a child's pose, yawned and then circled my feet as though nothing was wrong. I was standing there in tears, and all that time she had been hiding behind the washing machine, the one place I hadn't checked. I didn't think she'd fit in that skinny crevice.

Stupid me.

If I hadn't been so happy to see her, I would have fed her to the coyotes myself. Instead, I picked her up and squeezed her tight, smoothing her shiny black and white coat with my hand, and kissing the top of her head. She seemed irritated by the overwhelming show of affection, but at that point, I really didn't care.

A couple of nights later, somewhere around midnight, Chris texted again, this time with a picture of us holding hands in the U-Haul on the drive to San Diego. I did not see his message until the next morning, but I did respond.

Chris Hoyer

I want you back!!!!!

Book Girl Natalie
I'm struggling with this, Chris.

Chris Hoyer
Can I see you?

I still wasn't ready to see him. I was working it out in my head and in my in heart. Another day or two went by. I kept to myself, focusing on things I could control, like buying a new couch at Crate & Barrel, stocking the fridge with comfort food, buying a new Jeep and writing Love Notes. I traveled back and forth to the storage unit, pulling out everyday necessities that I could use around the apartment, stuff that I could actually lift on my own, like a spatula, my favorite Wolfgang Puck frying pan, and a few pretty decorative items. Except for a new couch, I didn't have any furniture, not even a bed. I gave it all away with the intention of buying all new stuff. I was living barebones for those first few days, and without Chris around, every room felt even more hollow. Even my phone seemed lonely. On the bright side, the cats were warming up to the new place, edging out of hiding and nosing around.

Somewhere in between, Chris checked in via text. He asked how I was doing, to which I responded with a photo of my new Jeep—no words, just the picture. I didn't have it in me to say anything more. Even though I may have rushed to judgement, I was hurt. And maybe it had more to do with my past pain than the present situation, but the feelings forced me to figure out what I wanted.

That Sunday afternoon, five days separating me from Chris, I headed to Carlsbad to take in the sunset. It was only a ten-minute drive. I needed a little ocean air. As I walked to my new Jeep, parked in my new parking space, I was taken aback.

For a second, I had to stop and think. What was happening? My brand-new Jeep was covered with envelopes, scores of them taped to the windows. I took a couple of steps closer, wondering what was going on, and then I knew. It was Chris's handwriting on the envelopes. He had done to me what I had been doing to so many others. He littered my car with Love Notes. One by one, I picked them off. There must have been at least thirty, including a small bouquet of roses tucked beneath the windshield wiper. When had he done this? How did he know? I scooched into the driver's seat—my hands full. I drove to the beach, copped a squat and opened them up, one by one.

The very first Love Note read: "I love you." My eyes instantly filled with tears. The second envelope had the extra key to his apartment, and the notes that followed were handwritten words describing me, including brave, future surfer, off the path, passenger, beautiful, sweet, smart, and the list goes on. I texted Chris a picture of the first Love Note, and I asked the question, "Do you?"

To which he replied:

Chris Hoyer

All the way!!!

I immediately got into my car and drove to him. Chris was waiting for me outside of his apartment complex, arms wide open. We held each other for the longest time, and he said the words out loud, "I *love* you! I *love* you! *You* are my dream girl, the dark-haired, green-eyed woman I have always daydreamed about."

He looked me in the eye when he said the words, and I believed him. The man does not do or say anything in haste. He is painstakingly precise in his actions. He doesn't have a reckless bone in his body, not when riding his motorcycle or handling his firearm, and certainly not when falling in love. In that moment, I knew everything was going to be all right because I knew him enough to know that he would not have said the words if he did not mean them.

That was the night "we" became "us."

Deep down I knew I was where I was meant to be. Chris felt the same way, too. To this day, he is convinced, had I not come into his life, he would be living alone, a terminally-single guy in San Diego.

"You are the only one for me, Nat. None of my friends or family could ever convince me to put myself out there again, until you. I don't want to lose you."

Swimming in the pool of his warm, brown eyes, I knew it was always leading up to this—to him. It took Chris and me a few days apart to figure out what "we" were. And what we were (are!) is a lot like what happens when the sun and the moon meet—magic! Albeit a little bit more down to Earth.

I love, love your story, Cuz! And I knew your mother so well, and right now she'd be saying, "That's my Natalie." She believed in you and all your dreams. We are so happy you found your fairytale and your knight in shining armor. I always enjoy your beautiful words.

—Bernadine S., Cousin

THIRTY-THREE
Cinderella Moment

G ratitude is the greatest godmother of all time. How do I know? Because when Mom and I first got into the "business" of writing Love Notes, I would often find myself wondering if I was really making a difference or if I was just squandering time. I asked God for a sign. I prayed for it. I said, "Lord, if this is what I am meant to be doing, please send me an invitation to a notable ceremony, like a policeman's ball."

I believe in asking big.

It didn't happen right away. Miracles take time. As it turned out, God was in the middle of writing my love story, as well as lining up my date for the big dance. I was patient and full of faith, and even though there were days my heart was breaking, and I was left wondering if what I was doing even mattered, I held fast to the belief that everything happens for good and that there was, indeed, a ball invitation with my name on it, and perhaps there would even be a handsome prince to boot.

The invitation came in the fall of 2019, just before I moved to California. It was a Policeman's Ball in Phoenix, Arizona. A Love

Note recipient (Gio) and his beautiful wife (Alex), extended the lovely invitation, and not a moment too soon. This was another of those "Aha" moments, the kind when you have to stop and pinch yourself. Not only had God responded to my prayer with a ball invite, but he included the prince as a part of the package.

I shopped for months to find the perfect dress for the policeman's ball and, of course, to scout out the perfect shoes. Mind you, I'm not one of those fashion plates who planned her wedding at the age of five years old or who spends hundreds of dollars at the salon. I am a simple girl—functional vs. fashionable. However, this was my "Cinderella Moment."

Everything had to be just right!

Days before the ball, I still hadn't locked down a pair of shoes to go with the dazzling navy-blue ballgown I bought. I dragged Chris around for an entire day searching high and low for the perfect shoe. I use the term "dragged" lightly, as Chris is always so patient, sweet and willing to tag along.

God love him.

I know the women in the shoe department at Macy's were smitten with him. There was an audible "Aww!" as they watched him kneel down, so to buckle every pair of shoes that I tried on. It's not that he has me *that* spoiled. It's just that I have a bad back stemming from all those years of being a single girl and having to do my own heavy lifting. We spent hours shopping for the right shoes and then, lo and behold, there they were! A cute kitten heel adorned with blue and clear glass beads.

They were perfect!

Fast forward to the night of the Policeman's Ball. Chris and I were getting ready in our hotel suite at the resort that was throwing the bash. I was in the bathtub, up-do and all, and as I soaped myself up, I started daydreaming about the dress, the dancing, the dinner and the …

Holy shit! The shoes!

I had forgotten to pack the shoes, the same shoes I had searched high and low for. My heart sank, as I let out a high-pitched shriek, "Oh! My! God!"

Chris burst through the bathroom door, braced for a fight, even if it meant squaring up to Norman Bates himself.

"What's the matter?"

"I forgot the shoes," I cried.

I cupped my face in my hands.

"Are you sure you didn't leave them in the car?"

"No," I pouted.

I was on the verge of tears, and that's when Chris went into hero mode. Grabbing the car keys from his pants pockets, he said, "I'll go look. You finish your bath."

If this man had been Clark Kent, this is the part where he would have unassumingly stepped into an empty phone booth, tore off his shirt and revealed the big "S" on his chest. As for me, I was a disaster. I lumbered out of the hot, soapy tub, like a grizzly bear that had just been shot with a tranquilizer. With barely enough will to wrap myself up into a bath towel, I fell back onto the bed and stared at the ceiling. I tried to remember the last time I had my hands on the sparkly size sevens. The ball was literally about to begin. I had less than thirty minutes to devise a plan, which wasn't looking good. Chris returned from the car *without* the shoes, and it looked as though I would, indeed, be going barefoot to the ball.

"Get dressed," he said. "There must be a shoe store somewhere nearby."

"There's no time," I whimpered, literally throwing in the towel and slipping into a pair of yoga pants and one of Chris' tee shirts. Kissing the crown of my throbbing head, he exclaimed, "We're not out of this yet!"

Chris wasn't exactly the "fairy godmother" we girls grew up with, not even close to what one might come to expect in such harrowing times as these, but who am I to look a gift horse in the mouth. The man was ready, willing and probably able to muster up a pretty pair of party shoes. So, in the car we go, and wouldn't you know it? We found a shoe store just three miles down the road. On top of which there was one pair of blue suede kitten heels that matched my dress. They were one size too big, but they were on sale and, moreover, there was no time to be picky. Needless to say, we bought the shoes and returned to the resort in record time. Chris showered while I dolled up. We walked through the big ballroom doors fashionably late by any princess' standards. I suppose if a girl is going to ask for a Cinderella moment, she should expect a major shoe snafu. However, if she plays her cards right, the hero (i.e., intrepid shoe locater) will swoop in and save the day.

The Policeman's Ball went off without a hitch. It was magical. It turned out to be something of a reunion for Chris, seeing so many of his friends and former colleagues that night. I could see in his face a sense of genuine appreciation for the positive reception *and* for my dress. Afterward, we slipped out of our formal wear and into our bathing suits. We poured ourselves into the resort hot tub—just the two of us. We owned the night, and just before climbing into bed, Chris ordered a movie on Amazon and then proceeded to gently pluck a million bobby pins from out of my up-do, one at a time. Thank you, Gio and Alex, for the fairytale invitation and for your friendship. Dreams do come true!

Hello, Natalie! I just wanted to reach out and say thank you!! You left a card on my Toyota Tundra yesterday outside Walmart. I found myself driving home with a tear slowly rolling down my face. I have never had a stranger do something like that for me. The thoughtfulness and time you take to do this is priceless and touched me in a place I often forget about. I genuinely appreciate your kind heart. Thank you for making a positive difference in my day!! You won't be forgotten!!

—John M., U.S. Military Veteran

THIRTY-FOUR

Return to Sender

O ne brisk November evening in 2019, we had just set up for a Love Note gathering on the outdoor patio of a local coffee shop, our first in California. Within our little circle was a handful of lovely ladies and, of course, Chris. He had come straight from work at the Marine base. He was still in uniform and was looking more like my personal security detail than one of our circle.

I had scouted the venue earlier that day and, as fate would have it, I left a Love Note for a Vietnam Veteran parked out front. I tucked the note into the sleeve of the driver side window.

Later that afternoon, the sun had begun its decent. Our little group of writing warriors made fun and friendly conversation while we penned love and gratitude to our nation's heroes. Not long into the event, a burly man with a formidable expression on his face deliberately stepped forward into our half-moon circle.

To look at him, you would have thought he had some sort of beef. He seemed so serious on the surface. The man reached for his pocket. Chris instinctively braced himself, leaning forward. From the corner of my eye, I saw him reach for his sidearm, something he no longer carried.

"I'm looking for Natalie," the man muttered, clutching an envelope that was addressed to a veteran. "She left this on my car this morning."

You could have heard a pin drop. I instantly stood up and replied, "I'm Natalie."

Chris edged himself closer to me, as the man took a hard step forward. That's when I noticed that his blue eyes were wet.

"My name is Creighton," he said. "I looked up your hashtag and saw on Facebook you were having a writing event."

He went on to share his story with us, beginning with what the Love Note meant to him and ending with his service in the Vietnam War.

"I am *so* happy my Love Note found you."

"Can I hug you?" he asked.

Before he could even finish his sentence, I landed one of *the* BEST and BIGGEST bear hugs of my life. Creighton, the Vietnam veteran, held me tight, his shoulders trembled as he wept in my arms. And, of course, I followed suit because in these arms, nobody cries alone. Truth: We were all in tears, the whole lot of us, even Chris.

It was extraordinary and yet another example of how love and kindness, when given freely, without expectation for anything in return, comes back to you—only magnified!

Since this mission began, I have held more of our nation's heroes in my arms than I can count, each dealing with demons brought home from their time in service, whether it was in war overseas or on the mean streets of America. The tears in their eyes tell me just how much they need this show of love, and the fact that many take the time to find me, so to thank me, reassures me that no good deed is ever wasted.

I want to thank you from the bottom of my heart. It was July 8, 2016. I was going through a very, VERY tough time. I was depressed. I was alone, and I needed something. I walked out of a movie theater and saw this [note] on my windshield. I felt loved and appreciated, even by a complete stranger. I cried, then smiled and lifted my head up. Thank you, Natalie! From what I can tell, you're the closest thing we have to a guardian angel.

—David S., U.S. Military Veteran

THIRTY-FIVE
Twist of Fate

O ver the last five-and-a-half years, I have tried really (REALLY!) hard to maintain a professional demeanor in my post as the Love Note Lady. It matters to me that people see me for who I am, a driving force for good. And since perception, like possession, is nine-tenths of the law, I do my best to keep my nose clean. The trouble is, when you hang around first responders (i.e., cops, hose draggers and the like), you quickly learn to expect the unexpected, and sometimes you have to risk reputation in order to preserve life, love, and the spirit of all that is good.

It goes with the territory.

Honestly, when Mom and I began this mission, I never dreamed it would go any further than handing out Love Notes to local veterans and first responders in the grocery store or while patrolling parking lots. If someone would have told me that I would be crashing the hospital room of an injured motorcycle officer just one day after he T-boned another vehicle during a pursuit, I would have told you that you had lost your mind.

Seriously.

Never in my life would I have believed that I would storm the hospital room of a complete stranger, let alone a law enforcement officer who, by the way, was fresh out of surgery. I have always made a concerted effort ***not*** to make people feel uncomfortable. More importantly, I never set out to get arrested while delivering Love Notes. However, one must be willing to risk such things if it's for the greater good. And this effort is all about the greater good. That said, let the record show that the following incident was ***not*** my idea.

In August 2019, nearly two years after I lost Mom, a Glendale motor officer was seriously injured while in pursuit of another vehicle. In the midst of that pursuit, a truck pulled out in front of him, causing him to T-bone. The officer was thrown from his mangled-up motorcycle, causing multiple serious injuries.

That same night, my Army veteran friend, Jeremiah, (i.e., Parking Lot Hug), happened to be on a police ride along with the local police department. He was riding with an officer named Ted, a good cop who just so happened to be best friends with the injured motor officer. The two went through the academy together. Upon hearing about his friend's accident, Ted was visibly upset. Because of that night's heavy workload, it was impossible for him to get to his best friend's side. As for Jeremiah, after hearing the news, he got busy texting me.

When I hear the words "We need Love Notes NOW," I go into autopilot. Within a matter of minutes, Jeremiah and I arranged for a Love Note writing session the following day. In that two-hour session, we collected over one-hundred Love Notes from coffee goers and baristas—everyone and anyone within arm's reach. On top of which, Starbuck's contributed a gift bag filled with coffee beans, gift cards and a reusable coffee cup. Chick-Fil-A also kicked in a big bucket filled with gift cards and goodies. There was only one question: How in the world would we get all of this Love Note loot to our injured officer?

Not wasting any time, Jeremiah pulled out his cell phone and made a quick phone call. Within a handful of minutes, no more than three, we had the name of the hospital AND the officer's room number.

"Let's go," Jeremiah exclaimed, placing all the goods into the back of his SUV. "He just got out of surgery."

"You're not serious!" I huffed.

"Oh, I'm dead serious!" Jeremiah laughed, ushering me into the passenger seat.

"We can't just storm this guy's hospital room. That is nuts!"

In the back of my mind, I imagined layers of police protection standing post, not to mention family and friends hanging around this officer's room. There was no way on God's green Earth we were getting anywhere near that guy, not without presenting some serious credentials or, as I mentioned, getting arrested.

"I know it's nuts," Jeremiah smiled. "That's why I love it!"

We loaded up, one of us apprehensively, and drove three miles down the road to the hospital. My heart was racing inside my chest. I was scared to death, but deep down I knew we needed to at least try. It was the right thing to do. I was sure, however, that we wouldn't get past lobby security, let alone the police protection perched outside of this man's room. To my surprise, there was none. In fact, the hospital staff didn't even question us.

As Jeremiah pushed through the officer's hospital room door, me, his wife and young son followed along behind.

"Yup! We're doing this," I whispered.

I held my breath, waiting for someone to give us a good what for—a nurse, a doctor, a cop, a storm trooper—somebody!

"I won't fare well in jail, Jeremiah."

"You're not going to jail," he laughed.

Was this really happening?

As we stepped inside the tiny room, pushing past the cubicle curtain that provided a small enclosure around the patient, I threw back my shoulders and smiled, as if we were meant to be there, as if I had any idea what the hell we were doing.

Confidence is key, even if only feigned for effect.

It was standing room only. There were no less than fifteen people surrounding the young officer. His baby face nearly made me cry. The young man was propped up in bed, pins and needles sticking out of him everywhere, and suddenly all eyes were on us. No one knew us from Adam, and yet we made our way through the crowded room, positioning ourselves at his bedside. Honestly, I was just waiting for someone to grab me by the scruff of the neck and toss me out on my ear, but that didn't happen.

"Hey," Jeremiah said, clearing his throat. "My name is Jeremiah, and this is Natalie, my wife and my son. We are with Nothing but Love Notes. We heard about your accident, brother, and we put together a little something for you."

Jeremiah placed the bucket of Love Notes on the foot of the bed, and as he continued to share our mission with the room, the looks of concern and confusion melted into something different, something warm and wonderful.

The young officer's name was Francisco. He broke down, unable to hold back the tears. It was beautiful. We shook some hands, managed some hugs and then walked out of that room with enormous grins on our faces (and without a restraining order). The world felt just a little bit better. I didn't know it at the time, but a seed of friendship had been planted.

Months later, I invited the two Glendale police officers, Francisco and his best bud Ted, to join us at a speaking event at a local high school. It was our second invitation to share our story with Westview's football program—150 male student athletes. I like to bring along a handful of my favorite first responders and Love Note writers to get up and share their Love Note story, speaking to the significance of this simple handwritten gesture. I believe it brings humanity to the table, a reminder that we are all human, and that these simple acts of kindness go a long way. Their stories give my story reason and listening to them never gets old. Nothing gives me more satisfaction than hearing how a Love Note saved the day!

Francisco, "Frankie," as we affectionately call him, shared his story of survival, beginning as a young man trying to find his feet in this world, hoping to break the "prison cycle" in his family. Frankie, also a US Army veteran, is a handsome young man with dark hair, friendly brown eyes, a square jaw and a million-dollar smile. He explained how much that bucket of Love Notes meant to his recovery and his goal of returning to the police force after his accident. He admitted that it was going to be a long road, but because of that special delivery, he felt motivated, if not inclined to return to a job he loved. Just as he was wrapping up, Ted chimed in, which took us all by surprise.

Ted spoke of fate and family and how we were all brought together by something greater. Ted hadn't always been a police officer. He was a mechanic for many years, and it was on *the* day of fallen Phoenix Police Officer David Glasser's funeral that Ted promised to do whatever it took to protect and serve his community. He was on his way to test for the police department that day. When he saw David Glasser's funeral procession, he pulled over onto the side of the road and respectfully waited for it to pass. That moment was a milepost for Ted.

And when he heard Chris' story, and learned his part in that important procession, in David Glasser's last call, he couldn't help but feel that fate had intervened and put us all together. There was not a dry eye in the house. It still gives me goosebumps as I write this.

One year later, Frankie flew out to San Diego to stay with Chris and me for a week. He had one final medical procedure to take care of before he could get back to the job. The surgeon was located in Los Angeles, and, of course, Chris and I offered to help him through it. There were several appointments leading up to the actual procedure, and because Chris was in between jobs, he was able to get Frankie to and from those appointments.

In between doctor visits, there was lots of beach time. One night the three of us went out to dinner with one of my favorite firefighter families. They were visiting California from Arizona. Ryan (a firefighter/paramedic/Love Note recipient), his wife Rebecca and their three awesome kids (Declan, Ethan and Ari) bought us dinner at our favorite pizza joint. Afterward, we all took a long walk along the beach, and all I could hope for was that somewhere out there, Mom could see the family I inherited because of our determination to spread love.

After Frankie's final procedure in LA, Chris drove him to

my place. It had been a long, busy week. Every day was a trip to Los Angeles. When the boys landed on my doorstep, I wasn't expecting to find Frankie doubled over in pain, groggy and nauseous from the anesthesia. If he had picked a fight with a wet noodle, I would have put my money on the noodle. Chris didn't look much better. He was exhausted from miles and miles of medical transport.

"You two look terrible," I said. "Did you lose a fight?"

"Feels like it," Chris said, kissing me on the cheek. "I'm going to go home, take a shower and throw on some fresh clothes. I'll come back later. We'll all crash here tonight."

"Oh, my goodness," I said, wrapping my arms around Frankie and leading him into my apartment.

Frankie leaned on me without saying a word. It was such a strange sensation, caring for this kid who we wouldn't have known, had it not been for a Love Note and the shameless act of crashing his hospital room. He was completely helpless, like a child, and he trusted us enough to put himself in our hands. The only thing I could think to do was to put him into bed and let him rest. He could barely move, and there was no better place for him. As I eased him onto the bed, he grimaced in pain. He was hurting.

"Are you hungry," I asked. "Can I make you some toast? How about some soup?"

Frankie declined at first. However, after a short nap and when the nausea subsided, he called out for me.

"Can I have some toast and soup?" he asked.

"Of course," I replied.

The truth is, it felt good to take care of him, to do our part in getting him back on his feet and whole again. It was a great privilege to see Frankie return to the force, and to see him get back on his motorcycle after that nasty accident. It wasn't easy for him, and there are still difficult days, but he keeps the faith, and he moves forward. That's all we can do—keep going.

I can't help but to believe that this was part of some divine plan, God entrusting Frankie to Chris and me. When it comes to mending our broken parts and those who are broken, we can't do everything, but we can do something, even if it's just a hot bowl of soup, a shoulder to lean on and the willingness to get arrested in the process.

I remember the day my husband received one of your notes. He came into show it to me, and he had a happier attitude for the entire day. The note made him feel as though not everyone out there hates the police! You are definitely making a difference—one card at a time.

—Cindy N., LEO Wife

THIRTY-SIX

God's Errands

I no longer believe in accidents. Everything (and everyone) happens for a reason. I believe that with my whole heart. In fact, there are days when I wonder if we aren't all just bustling around, running God's errands ... or the devil's, depending on who you talk to.

God has mind-blowing plans for each and every one of us, and if in our struggle and pain on Earth, we find it in ourselves to push through with faith, purpose and gratitude, there is life to be had beyond our wildest dreams. However, we must first stop and listen closely to our heart, so that we might hear that still, small voice inside of us. Call it our conscience, the moral GPS app that came with our original packaging at birth. *That* voice is what guides us in the right direction.

I tease about how Mom gave me a hard time about silly things, like love, lipstick and scrunchies, but the truth is she helped me tune into that small voice inside of me. When my brother and I were kids, she'd call us in off the street to tutor us on Bible verses and proverbs. She showed us what it meant to have faith and who we could lean on when life got hard. Of course, my brother and I didn't want to leave our friends to sit down with her for the thirty minutes she had carved out, but she insisted, and I'm glad she did.

Now—not so much then.

The trouble is, when life gets hard, it is all too easy to get distracted when left to one's own devices. We tend to get tangled up in stuff that numbs the pain, moves us away from the life we were promised, like alcohol, drugs, hate, social media and, well, you get the picture. Losing sight of one's purpose is, in my opinion, one of life's great tragedies. Purpose, in and of itself, is what gives our life meaning.

It redeems us.

After having spent two tiresome, albeit priceless years caring for Mom through cancer, I didn't know if I had it in me to survive her, but a Love Note saved me. The simple act of handwriting and delivering words of love and encouragement is what got me through it all—that and God's grace.

I can't say it enough.

There were days, however, when I'd wonder, if not question whether or not what I was doing made sense, and if it did, indeed, matter. I invested a great deal of my time, money and might into this little mission. More than anything, I wanted to know that these Love

Notes were landing in the right hands at the right time. That has always been the prayer.

One Saturday afternoon, Chris and I landed in a random parking lot in Point Loma, California. Knowing what I know now, I am convinced that there was nothing "random" about it. It had to have been meant to be. Chris and I had just spent the better part of the day ambling around the Rosecrans National Cemetery. If you haven't been there, it's worth the trip. It is a peaceful place overlooking the Pacific Ocean. So many of our nation's military heroes (and their loved ones) rest in that spot. With the smell of sea spray and freshly cut grass tickling our senses, we walked up and down the endless rows of American sailors, soldiers and the like who served and sacrificed so much. We even read some of their names out loud, wondering who they were and how they got there.

It was getting to be dinner time, so we loaded up into the Jeep and headed for home. It was Chris who noticed the lone police car parked in a lot on the opposite side of the street. Without warning, he made a hard U turn off of the skinny road and into the empty lot.

"What are you doing?" I asked, my right cheek planted against the passenger door window. I had been fiddling on my phone, so I had no idea.

"Ah," I smiled, seeing the patrol car parked by itself.

"Official Love Note business."

Have I mentioned how much I love this man?

Instinctively, I grabbed a Law Enforcement Love Note from my purse, praying that it had just the right message for this officer. As we approached the car from behind, I held my breath. It's always a little nerve wrecking walking up to a parked police car, especially from behind. It's kind of like stepping up to a horse from its hindquarters. You've got to let them know you're there—lest they get spooked, and you get your teeth kicked in.

Cops err on the side of caution. So, I try to be considerate of that. The officer rolled down his window and smiled cautiously as we approached. Most LEOs mistake Chris and me for lost tourists, a clueless couple seeking directions.

"Hello there," I said, smiling. "We just wanted to stop and say thank you for all that you do. We appreciate you. My son is a Texas sheriff's deputy and Chris (here) is retired law enforcement."

The officer grinned, "Well ... thank you!"

"This is for you," I said, handing him a Love Note.

The officer took the note. True to form, he was wearing dark sunglasses, but I could tell that he got a little misty, as he read the words (Thank you, Blue!) written on the envelope. It took him a moment to gather himself, but he thanked us both again.

"This means a lot," he said, clearing his throat and taking a deep breath. "My daughter was killed in the line of duty almost a year ago to the day."

Chris and I looked at each other, our eyes watering.

"What department was she with?" Chris asked.

"She was with the Honolulu Police Department."

The hair on my arms stood up. Chris and I knew exactly which officer he was speaking of. I remembered reading about her and her partner. They were two of 384 law enforcement line of duty deaths in 2020. I looked upwards toward the sky.

I see what You're doing.

"I'm sorry, brother ..." Chris exhaled. "Natalie sent a bundle of Love Notes to the department soon after that happened."

The officer nodded, clearing a frog from his throat.

"What's your name," I asked.

"Pete."

"I'm very sorry for your loss, Pete," I whispered.

And *there* it was ... the answer to my question.

It mattered.

Later that night Chris ran me a hot, Epsom-salt bubble bath. He even lit a few scented candles. My bath has always been my refuge, where I go to let down my guard—cry if I need to. I climbed into the hot tub of bubbles, and I broke, like a cheap bra.

Most nights Chris will pull up a seat on the floor next to the bathtub to keep me company. Some of our best conversations have happened there, but on that night, he stayed in the living room to tie up some loose ends. I was glad for the solitude. It gave me a chance to catch my breath and to say a prayer for Pete, his daughter, her partner ... and for my boy who was on duty in Texas that night. This Love Note hit close to home, too close for comfort.

I couldn't help but wonder how we came to find Pete in that parking lot—alone and so close to the anniversary of his daughter's death. I had to remind myself that I didn't need to know the how and the why.

"I know that was you, God," I said, in soft, muffled sobs. "*All* of this is you."

Honestly, if I had tried on my own to make any one of these connections happen, it would be next to impossible. It was only because of a Love Note that I made them. None of it was planned or thought out. It was pure, unadulterated blind faith, the act of writing Love Notes and trusting that they land in the hands and hearts that needed them most.

It was all because of God's grace. It was suddenly so clear to me. Had I stayed holed up on that lonely couch on Valentine's Day in 2016, held hostage by my own warped sense of fear and hopelessness, not one of these miracles would have happened. I wouldn't have met Chris. We wouldn't have published his book When *That Day Comes*. We wouldn't be in California—together.

When Mom was sick, I had so little control of my life. It was my lowest point. The only thing I could do was focus on the menial tasks involved with taking care of her: Bathing her, feeding her, washing her hair, getting her to her doctor appointments. Supplying her with her favorites—fudgesicles and homemade Rueben sandwiches.

Writing Love Notes to our nation's heroes was another simple task that I could take on. It took me away from much of the pain and fear I felt. I trusted God to take care of the rest—the BIG stuff.

And … praise God! He did … and then some.

I walked out to a handwritten note on my police Tahoe today at QT in Peoria. Just wanted to tell you how amazing that was and what an inspiration for all of the department. We aren't the heroes. People like you who selflessly do kind gestures like that for us, you, you are the heroes. Thank you for motivating us. Your kind notes are truly amazing.

—Eric M., Law Enforcement Officer

THIRTY-SEVEN
The Comeback

I t took on a life of its own. Our little Love Note story went viral. Who knew? What began as a run-of-the-mill Valentine's Day feel-good piece, turned into a social media sensation, giving Nothing but Love Notes its fifteen minutes of fame. It was a real boon to our little movement and to life, itself.

A pretty reporter named Brittni Thomason reached out from a local television news station in Phoenix. Being the fourth anniversary of our mission, she wanted to run a story that would feature the work we had done. I was living in San Diego at the time. However, I agreed to make the drive to Phoenix for the interview. While it wasn't our first news story or even our second or third, I felt it was important, if not fitting, since we had come so far since that momentous day on the couch on Valentine's Day 2016.

Chris and I made the trek back to the Valley. We crashed at Danielle's house the night before. She insisted. We got to spend some time with her and her family, which is always a good thing. She takes us in as her own. With a husband, four kids and as many dogs, it's what I would consider above and beyond the call of duty.

The morning of the interview, Chris and I met up with

Brittni and her camera guy in Buckeye, Arizona. For the record, there were no dumpsters involved. Thank goodness! However, my good buddy Zach, the Buckeye Police Sergeant, did come out and interview for the story. He's a *big* supporter of our little mission, and I couldn't love and appreciate him more for it.

Brittni was smitten with our love story, especially the sappy part about how Chris and I met and fell in love because of a Love Note. That "sap" became the hook, and the rest is history.

Chris and I drove home that same afternoon. While I was grateful for the news story and for being recognized for all of our hard work, I was just happy to be headed home to our little beach bungalow, none the wiser to what was about to happen.

A few days after our story aired, I received an email from a producer at The Today Show in New York City. That same afternoon, I got a call from another producer at Good Morning America. Within the next few months, media requests trickled in from CNN, Mike Rowe's Returning the Favor, The Kelly Clarkson Show, NBC San Diego and Woman's World Magazine. I even got a message from a radio station somewhere in Italy. Our love story was cropping up in my favorite newsfeeds: Tanks Good News, The Good News Network, Love What Matters, and The City of Kindness. The cherry on top was when Janice Dean, Fox News Senior Meteorologist and New York Times best-selling author, called to ask if she could write our Love Note Story in her next book, *Make Your Own Sunshine*.

Are you kidding me?

I was fielding phone calls almost every day from producers and journalists from across the country. I wondered: *What would Mom think about all of this?* Billy, my firstborn son, said it best. "Mom," he said. "I think she's the one behind it all."

It's funny, but life really is what *you* make it. It all comes down to having the courage to follow your heart, making the right decisions for *your* life and wellness and doing the work. On top of which, it's probably best to tune out the critics, and there will always be critics. Oftentimes, they come disguised as "friends" and family.

Don't let them get to you.

There are plenty of people out there rooting for you. We all experience tough times, and the pain and fear we feel is relative to where we are in our lives. However, in order to overcome, we must fuel our faith and power through. It is not for us to wonder how we will survive this life, only to have the faith that we will. You know that disclaimer engraved in the passenger side mirror of motor vehicles, the one that reads: *Objects in mirror are closer than they appear?* Well, the same is true of joy. It's closer than you think.

Don't give up hope!

For me, choosing to act vs. react to my circumstances is what made all the difference. It put me in a position of "superpower," as opposed to weakness. Knowing what I know now, I don't even want to think what my life would have looked like had

I not answered that "call to adventure," had I not acted.

In choosing to act from a place of love, I found my people, a tribe of real-life warriors who came through for me in ways I could never have imagined. These people, I call them my "Wolfpack," gave me the gift of love, support and encouragement. They restored my faith in all things good. They continue to show up for me (and each other) to this day, asking nothing in return. For that, I will spend the rest of my days trying to make it up to them.

They are my real comeback.

They fuel my faith and this mission by crafting homemade card stock, writing and delivering Love Notes, getting friends and family onboard, coming with me to share our love story at schools and businesses, giving me a soft place to land in my travels and on those tough days, and simply calling to check in on me.

That is what love looks like.

It looks like a woman named Maureen who spends a great deal of her time and energy creating amazing, customized Love Notes using fabric and cardstock—always adding our hashtag. I am blown away by her effort and willingness to contribute to this movement. It's people like her who make the world a beautiful place. My good friend Kary, a law enforcement wife, also makes the most beautiful handmade cards. Sometimes she even gets her badge-carrying hubby onboard. This beautiful mission has grown into something so much bigger than Mom and me.

It was destined to be.

Looking back at all of the time and money Mom and I spent

writing and hand delivering Love Notes to our nation's heroes, long before it was a thing, wondering if what we were doing was actually making a difference, I have to laugh. There were days, weeks and months when it was just the two of us, randomly littering love and gratitude around town. We would write until our hands hurt.

We were planting seeds.

Now that she's gone, I look around and I am surrounded by a garden variety of good people, the very community we showered with love. These good people whose hands and hearts now help to feed this mission are what grew from those "seeds." They are the better part of this love story.

In small measures, Mom and I could see the impact we were having on our hometown and, nearly every single day, we felt it. We just couldn't wrap our heads around its reach, until now. This Love Note mission began in desperate measure on a lonesome couch somewhere in suburbia. Honestly, it was really only meant to save her and me from the uncertainty we felt in the face of our own mortality. However, almost six years and more than 30,000 Love Notes later, collectively, it has become Hope's legacy.

People often respond to this mission as if Mom and I invented something as life changing as electricity, when all it really ever was … our inner light shining through in a tremendously dark place. Our setback, that "thing" meant to destroy us, suited up and made for a great comeback!

I've been hearing the words "guardian angel" a lot lately. Starting to think you are mine.

—Chris Hoyer, Law Enforcement Officer (RET).
& "The One"

THIRTY-EIGHT

Happily Ever After

C hris calls me his unicorn, but the truth is he is mine. Mom said men like him didn't exist, but that didn't keep me from believing for him. I held out for this man. I prayed for him, and I am so happy that I did. I can't imagine my life without him in it. We share a purpose. We are two peas in a pod, which is about the size of it, as we are shacked up together in a 600-square-foot apartment, sharing a washer and dryer with thirty other residents. On the bright side, and my whole point being, we are a ten-minute walk to the beach, and we are both free to pursue a beautiful life together.

We've never been happier!

On top of which, Chris makes me feel irresistible. Even on those days when I am least loveable, he wraps me up in his arms and kisses the crown of my head. He loves me unconditionally. Most days I prance around feeling and behaving much prettier and more precious

281

than I probably am in real life. I could literally roll out of bed with sleep in my eyes, a bad case of bedhead, monstrous morning breath and bloat from the beef and broccoli from the night before, and he'll look at me like I am magical, and he'll say something like, "Lady, you are too good to be true!"

And then, like an exclamation point at the end of that sentence, he'll kiss me twice—once on the lips and, so as not to make it feel left out, once on the forehead. He makes me feel safe and protected in every way a woman should feel safe and protected by the man she loves. Even on those nights when I steal the blankets or I have a bad dream, he is just one spoon away from a good night's sleep. It sure beats counting sheep. Chris is the most selfless man I know, most notably in the bedroom.

Did I say that out loud?

My only regret is that Mom is not here to see how this man loves and cares for her only daughter. No doubt she would have been keen on Chris, even though she and I had *very* different views on romantic love. Next to hair scrunchies, it was our biggest bone of contention, not to mention one of the reasons I likely remained single for so long after my divorce. I never wanted to disappoint her, not as a daughter and certainly not as the mother of her grandchildren. After she divorced my dad, Mom stayed single for the rest of her days, one and done. As for me, I never gave up on love. I held out for it. I believed that one day I would find it again, without having to settle.

Dust settles, not dreamers.

Mom used to give me a hard time about being such a romantic. She would say, "You're in love with love, Nat."

She may have been right about that, but after ending a nine-year marriage, I spent the next eighteen years proving my independence to her. A girl who was in love with love wouldn't have waited almost half her life to fall in love again, unless, of course, she was looking for the real deal.

For nearly two decades I put off having a love life for the sake of a good career, higher education, a home built from scratch, health benefits, two boys who grew up to be good men, if I do say so myself, and caring for her in the last two years of her life.

Even though I didn't anticipate those two decades whooshing by, I have no regrets, save a few lonely nights. But that's why God created Hallmark Christmas movies—the single girl's go to. Hey! You do what you got to do to get through, especially during the holiday season. While I wasn't foolish enough to believe that life and love could be as picture perfect as those found in schmaltzy Christmas movies, I had good reason to believe for the happy ending. And I do believe I found one in the breadth of my mission. Chris asked me to move in with him in March of 2020. With one dusty, old box fan and two tuxedo cats, we are living our best life!

One afternoon Chris and I were walking along the boardwalk at the Hotel Del in Coronado. It was the middle of November, and I was telling him how much I loved romantic Christmas movies during the holidays. I looked up at him, smiled, and said, "I want to live in a Hallmark Christmas movie."

Chris, a man's man, a guy who considers Bruce Willis' Die Hard *the* quintessential Christmas movie, rolled his eyes and chuckled. He grabbed my hand, pressed it hard to his lips and said, "Natalie, your life *is* a Hallmark Christmas movie."

From his lips to God's ears.

In writing and inspiring thousands of Love Notes to our nation's heroes, I had unwittingly written my way into an epic love story. With a little help from above and barrels of ink, I penned my own happy ending! I got the beach, the boy and now the book, and it was all because of a Love Note. Feeling nothing but love and gratitude in my heart, I looked up to the bright, blue sky that day and whispered a prayer into the salty, sea breeze, those two modest, but mighty words that saved my life.

"Thank you!"

The End

The Last Love Note

One night Chris and I were walking along Moonlight Beach. We were headed home after eating at our favorite pizza place. It was dark, and a thick marine layer was slowly edging its way inland, eating up the stars in its path. The harvest moon was big and bright, casting sparkling diamonds across the water's surface. It was magical. Holding hands, we walked for a good mile without saying a word. There was something soothing in our shared silence.

I was happy … happier than I had been in a long time. I got to thinking about Mom and what she'd think about me being here on this beach, holding hands with this man. After she was called Home, I secretly hoped that I would find one last Love Note from her, one last letter that would give me hope that everything would be all right and that I would find happiness again. When I cleaned out her room, I thought I might find a note hidden somewhere in her jewelry box, tucked in a pillowcase or folded inside of the pages of a book. Even though there was nothing she could have said that she hadn't already said, I held out hope for one last connection with her.

"I wish Mom had left me one last Love Note before she died," I said, breaking the silence.

Chris looked at me with such love in his eyes. Not knowing what to say, he smiled softly, squeezed my hand and kissed the crown of my head. That gesture said more to me than words could say. I wondered if, somewhere out there, Mom could feel how happy her daughter was, knowing how much her love and influence had to do with that. I missed her so much. My eyes began to water, so I let go of Chris' hand and strayed toward the ocean's edge. The cool tide rolled in, rushing over my bare feet. We walked another fifty yards or so, and suddenly Chris called out to me.

"Hey, Nat!" he shouted. "Come here."

Taking out his pocket flashlight, he shined the light down at his feet. Written in the sand was the word "HOPE" in big, bold letters and outlined in rocks below it was a peace sign and the shape of a heart. My heart caught in my throat, and I started to cry, like a baby. Chris wrapped his arms around me and held me tight, as I sobbed into his chest. Could it have been the one last Love Note from Mom? Knowing her and seeing her name scrolled there in the sand, I believe it was. With that last sand-written Love Note and every single apple sticker that I see, I think of her and smile. I imagine she is somewhere out there smiling, too, ever so aware that her daughter is happy, loved and very much at home in her life. Honestly, I'm not convinced that she didn't have a hand in it. When it came to me, her only daughter, she always did.

A Love Note saved my life, a simple paper container with a sealable flap that holds a little bit of hope for our everyday heroes. It was the gateway to creating a more meaningful life, personally and professionally. And thanks to this little mission, I saw my dying mother come to life in her last two years on this earth. I have seen grown men melt with just a few handwritten words of thanks. I have witnessed miracles, big and small. I have fallen in love with people from all walks of life, friends I would never have known, had I not answered life's call to adventure. When it comes to life and the people in it, always go the extra mile. Save a few blisters and a broken heart, I can tell you, *that* is where the magic is.

Looking at my life today, I can't help but smile. I am a ten-minute walk to the beach. I am living with the man of my dreams. I am happy and without regret. I believe this has everything to do with a life lived in gratitude—matched, of course, with my innate gluiness. Gratitude, gluiness and
God's grace saved me. It got me through my darkest days, but it was

a handwritten Love Note and a mother's love that pushed me forward into the fray, moved me away from my pain and into the heart of an epic love story.

It was all because of a Love Note.

My dear friend, Carol Latham, believes it was so much more than that. And, to some extent, she is right. It took a whole lot of guts and gumption to push this envelope, and it wasn't without extreme effort. It certainly didn't happen without a lot of persistence and help from good people like you, dear reader. However, because it originated from the heart and because the work felt so good, it may have seemed more like a cake walk.

Here's the thing: Life is hard. It genuinely sucks sometimes, but with prayer, purpose, faith, love, and gratitude, it can be good again. On those days when everything goes pear shaped, take comfort in knowing that our time here on Earth has meaning and that, at the end of the day, the life and love we make is not for nothing, so long as we are purposeful in our endeavor. I am convinced that the good you do for others, whether you feel they deserve it or not, can't help but find its way back to you—only packaged so much prettier. If you don't believe me, give love away without condition. See for yourself. Gratitude changes everything!

For the better part of my life, I dreamed of and even prayed for a love story of this caliber—and it *is* a love story, on so many levels. I just never expected it to come at such a great toll. But then again, if you look back through the course of history, the greatest love stories always do.

"Natalie, maybe the reason I'm always giving you a hard time about your being a romantic is because that is what I envy the most about you."
—Mom, Valentine's Day 2017

P.S. Thank you for leaving me a "Love Note" on Amazon reviews!

xoxo

ACKNOWLEDGEMENTS

Thank You!

This book is a love letter to all those who showed up in my life (and stuck around) because of a Love Note. There are no words to express my gratitude for each and every one of you, except to say, "Thank you!" You helped fuel my faith on this great, big adventure that took me from heartbreak to hope to happiness.

On that first drive home from the hospital at 2 a.m., I was alone, and I didn't know how I would ever say goodbye to Mom. She was my best friend and the strongest woman I knew. I also had no idea that God had so many new hellos up His sleeve, good people to pull me through to the other side of this epic love story. He introduced me to my proverbial pack, and it changed my life—forever! Seneca, the Roman Stoic philosopher, put it best. He wrote, *"Throw me to the wolves, and I will return leading the pack."*

I love that, and I absolutely love my Wolfpack! Thank you for loving and supporting me every day. I lost one of the great loves of my life, and in (merciful) return, God personally gave me each one of you. I can honestly say, hand over heart, that the power of the wolf is in the pack, and the power of this epic love story is in each of you, happily ending with the good man I prayed so hard for.

Chris Hoyer, something tells me God smiled the day we met. He knew, long before we did, that you and I would end up together by our beach and in our book *When that Day Comes: Training for the Fight*. Getting here wasn't easy for either one of us, but there was never any doubt that it would be "you and me" in the end. You are every bit the good man I prayed for, and I am blessed to be the one by your side. Thank you for loving me, for pushing me, and for running my bath at the end of a long day. *You* are my best!

And to those who have shown up for me in big and small ways, you are my kind of company, the kind a girl keeps close to her campfire: Alec Reilly, Billy & McKenzie Reilly, Eli Reilly, Asher Reilly, Nathan & Jennifer Hirni, Alexis Hirni, Chase Hirni, Lila Dominguez, Bernadine Schmaltz, Donna Broders, Brenda Fick, Steve & Debbie Swenerton, Neilie Johnson, Billy & Noreen Allsop, Erin Allsop-Arcuri, Kaitlin Santisteban, Claire Reilly, Alex Hoyer, Cassandra Hoyer, David Glasser #8144, Bob Duffy, Carol Latham, Jeremiah & Bryson Thompson, Zach Astrup, Elise & Brad Alexandra, Danielle & Chris Villa, Chloe Villa, Andie McCormick, Frankie Villa, Cayden Villa, Brian Holbert, Sherri Holbert-Bartish, Wyatt Bartish, Ryan Rodriquez, Rebecca Rodriquez, Francisco Martinez, Ted Venable, Rich Stringer, Alex & Gio Minera, Macy Mortensen, Colleen Koblinski, Brad Lerman, Rich & Kary Pfeifer, Patrick & Sarah Crouse, Arial Hastings, Alan & Linda Pfohl, Nick Gerhts, Nyanna Stumpp, Tiffany Stumpp, Mylinda Fine, Natalie Stahl, Andrea & Brendan Austin, Maria & Donnie Banowiecz, Renee Damon, Creighton Lawhead, Chris Stevens, Janice Dean, Governor Doug Ducey, Vice Mayor Jon Edwards, Mayor Cathy Carlat, Terry Skinner, Sara & Jon Correll, Dave

Weiner, Chris & Elizabeth Gregario, Chrissy Glunt, Geneen Kudler, Roger Sandeen, Brad Kudler, Michael McInnis, Ryan Jacques, Chelsea Opat, Amanda Stjernholm, Teri Lauderdale,   Christine Ursich, Candace O'Connor, Thomas Yoxall, Phil Claxon, Scott McAllister, Shawn Magness, Presley Symington, Gracie Swift, Brandy Green-Hansen, Diane Olesky Johnson, Kelly Hamper, Maureen Pierce, Pat & John Harrington, Annie Vaughn, Dave Zussman, Erika Iglesias-Colon, Brian Osborn, Edith Tilden, Nancy Garren, Davita Solter, Bonita Simpson, Sarah Harris, Lori Jacques, Charlotte Boland, Tirzah Jankowski, Gillian Grim, Hope Baena, Melissa Johnson, Pam Crow, Geordan Key, Caroline, Marty, Leah & Bradley Berger, Jessica Graves, Miriam Hoffmaster, The Bigelow Family, Alayna Jacobson, Tricia Quezada, Charley's Heroes, Ken Riege, Hiroshi H. Miyamura, Sandee Lee Giller, Wendy Hunt, Kelly Meyer, Betty Rushlow, Brownie Troop 1639, Heather Dinges, DeeAnn McGarey, Victor Ingalls, Christine Johnston-Klauschie, Kathy Cutino Palmer, The Wright Family, Denice Heintz-Tomlinson, Dean Tomlinson, Jill Fuqua, Amanda Goodman, Brittni Thomason, Lexie Max, Jennifer Getchell, Centennial High School, BGRS, Arizona Ice—Peoria, Daughters of the American Revolution—Piestewa Peak Chapter, Peoria Police Citizens Academy Alumni, Peoria Police Department, Peoria Fire Department—Station 195 & 193, Starbuck's P83, Athletic Ink, S&S Tire, Westview Knights Football, Verrado High School, Desert Edge High School, Team Bad Axes, Pam Hudgins & St. Thomas the Apostle School—Phoenix, Grandma's Restaurant—Oceanside, Kelly Clarkson, Good Morning America, CNN, Woman's World magazine, Localish, Z93 Outlaw Country and to every one of you who has put forth the ink and the effort to spread love in the name of Nothing but Love Notes. It was a dying woman's wish that we keep going, and I am grateful for all of the hands and hearts who helped make it happen!

Natalie June Reilly is a freelance writer, mother, grandmother and every bit her mother's daughter. She is the founder of Nothing but Love Notes, a movement that has inspired a generation of love and gratitude across the country. Somewhere along the way, Natalie unearthed her happy ending, unwittingly landing the beach, the boy and now the book. Nothing in the pages of this epic love story would have been possible, if not for God's grace, a mother's love and, of course, a handwritten Love Note.

Works Cited

Ballerini, Kelsea. June 7, 2017. *Legends.* Comp. Kelsea Ballerini.
Petty, Tom. October 27, 1989. Free Fallin'. Tom Petty & Jeff
Lynne.

Center for Disease and Control. Accessed November 1, 2021.
https://www.cdc.gov/suicide/pdf/preventing-suicide-
factsheet-2021-508.pdf.

Photographs:

Page 15, Billy Reilly & Hope Hirni

Page 16, Hope Hirni & Natalie Reilly

Page 17, Hope Hirni

Page 29, Jeremiah & Bryson Thompson

Page 30, Ryan Jacques

Page 45, Bob Duffy

Page 48, Carol Latham & Natalie Reilly

Page 53 & 54, Elise Slagle & Natalie Reilly

Page 64, Michael McInnis

Page 67, Ryan Rodriquez & Natalie Reilly

Page 85, Hope Hirni

*Page 105, Natalie Reilly, Gio Minera, Jeremiah Thompson, Brad Lerman,
Zach Astrup, Christine Johnston-Klauschie, Colleen Koblinski, Shawn
Magness, Ryan Rodriquez (Photo taken by Miriam Hoffmaster)*

Page 109 & 113, Nyanna Stumpp

Page 128, Elise Slagle, Amanda Stjernholm & Natalie Reilly

Page 129, Ariel Hastings, Elise Slagle & Amanda Stjernholm

Page 139, Zach Astrup & Natalie Reilly

Page 142, Zach Astrup, Natalie Reilly & Jeremiah Thompson

Page 150, Alan Pfohl & Natalie Reilly

Page 155, Elise Slagle & Natalie Reilly

Page 159, Debbie Edenhofer & Natalie Reilly

Page 162, Sherri Holbert-Bartish & Wyatt Bartish

Page 170, Chloe Villa, Andie McCormick, Danielle Villa & Natalie Reilly

Page 174, Brian Osborne & Chase Hirni

Page 175, Zach Astrup, Colleen Koblinski, Natalie Reilly & Jeremiah Thompson

Page 215, Roger Sandeen & Natalie Reilly

Page 224, Natalie Reilly & Chris Hoyer

Page 231, Kevin Pohlman, Sergio Tosi, Nik Gazda, Natalie Reilly & Brad Lerman

Page 254 & 255, Creighton Lawhead & Natalie Reilly

Page 263, Francisco Martinez, Chris Hoyer, Natalie Reilly, Declan Rodriquez, Rebecca Rodriquez, Ryan Rodriquez, Ari Rodriquez & Ethan Rodriquez

Page 265, Chris Hoyer, Natalie Reilly & Francisco Martinez

Acknowledgements, Zach Astrup, Shawn Magness, Brad Lerman, Gio Minera, Natalie Reilly, Christine Johnston-Klauschie, Jeremiah Thompson, Colleen Koblinski & Ryan Rodriquez (Photo by Miriam Hoffmaster)

Made in the USA
Columbia, SC
22 March 2022

58006046R00193